W9-CZN-953

The Third Book of THE ADVENTURES OF A FEDERAL AIR MARSHAL

HIRED TO SERVE

Love you Mary Ann.
Madelyn

MADELYN I. SAWYER

outskirtspress
DENVER, COLORADO

The opinions expressed in this manuscript are solely the opinions of the author and do not represent the opinions or thoughts of the publisher. The author has represented and warranted full ownership and/or legal right to publish all the materials in this book.

Hired To Serve
The Third Book of the Adventures of a Federal Air Marshal
All Rights Reserved.
Copyright © 2015 Madelyn I. Sawyer
v1.0

Cover Photo © 2015 thinkstockphotos.com. All rights reserved - used with permission.

This book may not be reproduced, transmitted, or stored in whole or in part by any means, including graphic, electronic, or mechanical without the express written consent of the publisher except in the case of brief quotations embodied in critical articles and reviews.

Outskirts Press, Inc.
http://www.outskirtspress.com

ISBN: 978-1-4787-5283-7

Library of Congress Control Number: 2015903716

Outskirts Press and the "OP" logo are trademarks belonging to Outskirts Press, Inc.

PRINTED IN THE UNITED STATES OF AMERICA

To: The FAMs I flew with, the FAA colleagues I worked with, and the many friends I cherish.

Contents

CHAPTER 1

Airport on Lockdown

"Go. Go. Go," yelled the man on the phone. My ears were ringing, not only from the harsh sound of his high pitched, panicked voice, but from the annoyance that he had the audacity to think that I wasn't already on the move. Simultaneously listening, talking and driving my car, I was racing to the airport without benefit of a siren or flashing lights on the roof of my personal vehicle. Jerry Johnston, or JJ as we call him, had already contacted me about the security incident unfolding at the Los Angeles International Airport (LAX). The details were thin, but when JJ calls from the operations center with an emergency, it's time to roll. So I was breaking every traffic law, and with a blast of my horn, running every red light between Redondo Beach and the airport. I was racing against time, and time was already far, far ahead of me.

Okay, now I was officially annoyed. I continued to listen to the shrill voice dictating orders to me as if he could do any good 2300 miles away in Washington, D.C. In reality, I was more annoyed that they were second guessing my every move because I was the field agent responding directly to the situation, and they were only the D.C. desk wonks dictating orders.

Calm down, Maggie, calm down. I know they don't get it. Worse, they don't get that they don't get it. I felt slightly more entitled to be critical, having spent three years in D.C., as a staffer, spending many an hour listening to management pontificate about field incidents when they themselves had never served in the field. It hit a raw nerve with me since I'd been there and done that--both as a field agent, a staffer in D.C., and now as a senior field agent. I was experiencing, once again, the direct effects of D.C. trying to control a situation in which they had no control whatsoever.

The duty officer, JJ, and I knew each other very well by now. When I became the Los Angeles Civil Aviation Security field office (CASFO) manager in July 1995, I personally went to the Regional Operations Center to meet the men and women who worked the console there. During their twelve hour shifts they filtered through telephone calls, email messages, and televised events, notifying managers, supervisors, and other employees who were on call about events or emergencies impacting their work areas. If any employee had to be on top of their game every day, and be able to multi-task it was this team. And JJ was the best of the best.

With the LAX CASFO being the largest CASFO, its geographical area covering sixteen airports, over fifty large and small airlines, a multitude of airport security checkpoints, and forty-seven special agents, security incidents and breaches were going to happen. During my first year as the manager I wanted the operations center to call me directly in the event of a security-related incident at any of my airports. This amounted to my being on duty 24/7, being notified and responding to airport and airline incidents.

Heck yeah, I knew it was a crazy idea. I said this to myself every time my phone rang, especially in the middle of the night or on a weekend. Yet there was no better way to learn my airports and all the hundreds of contacts if I didn't. So I personally answered telephone call after telephone call and responded to incidents in person.

And this Saturday morning proved to be no different as I raced toward the airport with D.C. management buzzing in my ear, while JJ kept the open conference call connected and secure. He was my silent partner in this and every incident to which our security field office responded.

Turning left onto Century Boulevard from Aviation Boulevard my Jeep Cherokee skidded through the yellow light, the tires groaning as I flattened them against the pavement, twisting the wheel hard to the left, and then centering it as I raced toward the main entrance to the airport. Fortunately, the traffic into the airport was minimal this morning. God must have known I needed a break because once I turned onto Century Boulevard, every light stayed green as I zoomed toward the United Airlines terminal located at the farthest end of the enormous circular terminal.

Thank you, Lord, I said to myself as I cleared each traffic light and moved deeper into the central terminal area. As I neared Terminal five, then six I began to see crowds of people: passengers, airline personnel, and police spilling off the sidewalk and into the street.

"I'm here. I'll get you a situational status report as soon as I can. JJ, I'm signing off now, but I'll call back as soon as I find out what's going on."

"Roger that," JJ said.

"Yes, call us immediately," D.C. chimed in as I hit the call end button on my phone.

I stopped in front of terminal five, parked my car curb-side, rolled up my windows, threw my FAA placard on the dashboard, and began running toward terminal seven.

"Well, well, what's going on?" I said aloud. I had replaced the cell phone I'd been holding in my left hand with my Federal Aviation Administration (FAA) special agent credentials as I quickly assessed the situation. I knew I was about to get into a shoving match with hundreds of people, inside and outside the terminal, who were now wall to wall, stuck together like sardines in a can, and not looking very happy. The California sunshine was beginning to break through the morning gloom which, I knew, would make the situation even more unpleasant for everyone stuck outside.

I looked up toward the screening checkpoint located on the second level and saw the same mass of passengers stuck in place.

"FAA Security, FAA Security, coming through," I shouted as I held my credentials above my head and began pushing through the thick crowd.

A few feet ahead of me I saw an LAX Airport police officer doing the same thing I was, pushing, shouting, and shoving his way through the crowd. He was taller and wider that I was, plus he had a recognizable police uniform on versus my FAA navy blue security shirt and Levis.

I had an idea and it was--a good one.

So I quickly pushed my way toward the officer; after stepping on sandaled toes, tennis shoes, business loafers, and boots, I stepped directly behind him and followed him through the maze of people. Our common goal was to get to the checkpoint ASAP.

"FAA Security behind you," I shouted out.

Looking back the officer saw my credentials, did a quick head nod, and off we went up the down escalator, pushing, stomping, and moving at a snail's pace into the now impatient crowd of passengers stuck in line on the second level. The crowd was so thick you couldn't see the security checkpoint, but I knew it was just a few yards away.

Finally we arrived at the checkpoint.

"Who's in charge? And what's going on?" the officer asked in a growl of a voice to the first screener he saw.

"FAA Security," I said with an equal growl.

When the screener turned around I immediately noticed his ashen skin and the perspiration beading up on his face. His hand trembled as he raised his arm and pointed at the tunnel of the x-ray machine.

"Look, look, I think it's a bomb," he said, fortunately, in a low hushed voice.

The officer and I rushed over to the x-ray machine monitor and looked at the image. Clearly it was the image of a bomb: wires, two rectangles that looked like dynamite, and a battery.

"Shit. Who put this bag on the belt? Do you know who?" I asked.

"No, I'm not sure now, we were so busy, but we told everyone to stay in place after we saw it," the screener said shakily. "If I had to guess, those two people right there are closest to the x-ray machine. I think it's them."

"Let's go," the officer said, grabbing me by the elbow.

"In the meantime, close off this area immediately." The officer pointed to our left and said, "Flow those passengers up the stairs and into the parking garage."

"Yes, sir," the screening manager said. He had just arrived at the checkpoint. I saw him approach a few minutes earlier while we were talking to the screener.

Good, but where was Stanton? Agent Stanton was the focal point for all security matters at LAX, and I didn't see him yet, which worried me. I quickly called JJ back, asking him to page Agent Stanton.

Better to be called twice than not at all.

Agent Stanton was the Federal Security Manager (FSM) for LAX. The FAA had finally awakened in the early 1990s after years of having serious attacks and threats directed at U.S. airlines, both internationally, domestically, and at some airports. When these threats occurred, the FAA would mandate additional security measures to be implemented. When the airports and airlines had to implement those measures the biggest complaint by the regulated parties was there was no focal point with whom they could discuss implementation. After years of heated debates the Congress and the President mandated by law that the FAA appoint a manager for the largest airports. Those managers' sole responsibility would be to oversee the security posture of the airport and their tenant airlines. The FSM was FAA Security's representative and answered directly to FAA headquarters in Washington, D.C. I didn't directly report to Stanton, but for all security matters he was the final authority at LAX. We worked well together and I didn't like the fact that he wasn't here.

Other officers were beginning to arrive; the LAPD bomb squad had been notified and was responding. The slow flow of passengers away from the checkpoint had begun. It was bedlam! Inconvenienced passengers were yelling, security screeners and airline personnel were trying to appease them, but in reality the only thing they wanted was to get through screening and head for their flights.

The only good thing about the situation, so far, was the press hadn't arrived. But it would only be a matter of time before they did.

Walking over to the two passengers standing near the x-ray machine I felt my gut tighten slightly in anticipation of what potentially could happen. There were two individuals: a man whose eyes were covered with aviator shaped silver rimmed sunglasses, and a woman with similar glasses on top of her head, holding her hair back away from her face.

"Hello, I'm Officer Kennedy, Airport Police, and this is Special Agent Stewart from the FAA."

"Yes?" said the man in a questioning tone, pulling his sunglasses on top of his head, similar to his traveling companion.

"Is that your bag in the x-ray machine?"

"I believe it is, at least our bags haven't come out yet. Why? What's the matter?"

"I need you two to follow me now."

The four of us walked over to the police podium, a fixed post located beside the checkpoint, but with clear visibility of the entire area. Two other officers at the podium stood nearby along with the security checkpoint supervisor and a United Airlines manager.

"I need both of your identifications," Officer Kennedy stated.

Presenting foreign passports and their airline tickets, the two began explaining who they were, what they were doing in the U.S., and where they were going.

"We're part of a film crew working on a documentary about the Unabomber for the BBC in London. We just finished up shooting here. We're heading back to London this afternoon."

"Oh my God, I know what's happening," the woman suddenly said. "It's our equipment isn't it? That's what you're looking at in the x-ray machine, right?"

"What do you think we're looking at? What's in there?" I asked.

"We're shipping some of our props home in our carry-on luggage so they don't get lost," she said.

"The replacement costs would be enormous," the man said. "The replica book bomb is there in the x-ray machine."

"We've got the bomb squad responding now, so we're all going to sit tight and wait here."

The man and woman took a seat on the metal bench beside the police podium looking both scared and annoyed--scared that they were going to get arrested, and annoyed because by now they had figured out that they were probably going to miss their flight.

"I'm going to head back over to the checkpoint."

"Okay, Stewart."

The airline manager and screening manager had already returned to the checkpoint and were talking to a few of the screeners who waited anxiously for the bomb squad to arrive.

The passengers had been cleared off the second level, but the main United Airlines Terminal lobby was jam-packed, wall to wall, with passengers who were not at all pleased with the circumstances. And there was virtually no place to go. No one could move – it was a mess.

I pulled my cell phone from my back pocket and called JJ.

"Operations Center, JJ speaking."

"JJ, its Maggie. Can you connect me with the Washington Operations Center? I've got an update for them, and would you stay on the line so you can hear what's going on too."

"Roger that. Stand-by, calling D.C. now," he said.

"Washington Operations Center, go ahead with your SITREP," the dull, bored bureaucratic voice said.

"This is an update to my initial call-in this morning that a suspicious item was in one of the x-ray machines at the United Airlines Terminal security checkpoint. Terminal seven, on the upper level has been closed. All of the passengers have been evacuated from the upper level, the bomb squad is responding, and two individuals have been detained and identified as having knowledge about what's in the x-ray machine."

"Go on."

"Two individuals, a man and a woman, were filming a documentary on the Unabomber and it's believed that some of their prop--a replica of a book bomb, to be specific--caused a screener to call for LEO support at the checkpoint."

"The two individuals have advised the police, and me, that the prop in the x-ray machine looks very real."

"Roger that," D.C. said.

"The bomb squad is on their way. No press, yet. And the checkpoint is secure."

"I've got to hang up now. I see the bomb squad downstairs coming into the building now."

"JJ, are you still there?"

"Sure am."

"That's all we have right now. In case the press starts calling, just tell them the local authorities and FAA are onsite. K?"

"Roger that. And Stanton is rolling. No one notified him, and man-oh-man is he pissed."

"Thanks for finding him JJ. I'm signing off. I'll call back after the bomb squad reports."

I heard Stanton before I saw him, his commanding voice booming through the terminal like a bass drum's music bouncing off the walls inside a car. Stanton wasn't angry, but I knew him well enough that I could tell he was frustrated to hear about this incident in an untimely manner.

As he walked up and stood beside me, we both saw the Los Angeles County Bomb Squad arrive.

"Thanks for the heads-up; damn D.C.," Stanton said.

"Thought so, glad I called."

As we rested our hands on top of the metal balcony rail, I quickly brought him up to speed. We watched the bomb squad weaving their way through the main lobby as Officer Kennedy and I had earlier. The thick dense crowd of humanity did their very best to get out of the way but multiple toes, shoes, and boots were tread upon as if they were the flooring.

"How'd you get up here?" I asked Stanton.

"After setting my own personal speed record to get here, I came through the parking garage on the second level. JJ told me the terminal was a madhouse."

"God bless JJ."

"Yep, he's one of the best," Stanton said.

The bomb squad team got off the escalator and briskly made their way to the security checkpoint. Officer Kennedy briefed them and they immediately cleared the area and went to work.

It took the team about fifteen minutes to determine the device in the x-ray machine was inert. Stanton stayed at the checkpoint to restore order while I went with the bomb squad to collect their names and take pictures of the book bomb.

"Pretty realistic isn't it?"

"Sure is," I said to the officer.

We exchanged business cards so our reports would have the correct responder and contact information.

"We'll be hanging onto this baby for a long time. It's so realistic. It will make an excellent training tool for us."

The officer placed the device on the hood of his police car while I snapped a few photos of it for the enforcement investigation reports or EIRs that I knew I would be writing very soon. I had already decided earlier that I was going to handle this myself rather than handing the information off to one of my agents in the office to write. It had gotten too much attention from the folks in D.C. so I knew it was already a high priority on their list – like a Monday morning priority.

Oh well, that's why I made the big bucks. I shook the officer's hand, thanked him for his rapid response time, and went back to the security checkpoint to find Agent Stanton standing over the two passengers who owned the fake device.

CHAPTER 2

Agent Lee Stanton

"I'm the Federal Security Manager, Agent Stanton for the Los Angeles International Airport. Who are you two?" he said with his distinctive deep calm voice that always commanded attention. His voice dripped authority.

He was well over 6'2", not slim, not fat - just bulky. He was a grizzly--rugged like John Wayne – always in control, always on the lookout, and always strutting his slightly rebel side. You either loved him or hated him. He didn't cut anyone any slack. If you did your job he'd tell you so and if you didn't do your job he'd tell you so.

I'd known Stanton for years now. He hadn't changed a bit except a few loop holes on his belt. He was the first partner I had when I joined the federal air marshal cadre. We trained together, flew together, and worked together.

I could hardly bear to watch in anticipation of what I knew would happen. But I couldn't help myself. So I walked up and stood beside him.

"Special Agent Stewart, we met earlier," I said.

"So what happened?" Stanton asked.

As they explained their story I took notes. Stanton fired away question after question, seemingly not satisfied with their responses or their attitudes.

"Do you know how many federal regulations you two violated today?"

They looked puzzled. They clearly did not understand the severity of what they had done.

"Well, for starters Federal Aviation Regulation 108.11 (d) which is carrying a deadly or dangerous weapon, concealed or unconcealed, through the checkpoint, which would be accessible to either of you once you are onboard your flight," Stanton told the now-stunned couple.

After spending about an hour together, Agent Stanton turned to the police officer standing nearby and advised him that he didn't have any further questions.

"We're booking them?" the officer asked.

"Works for us," I said. "We're opening a civil enforcement investigation against them."

"Let's go. We have a few more questions for you."

Protesting their rights as journalists, they ultimately stood up, the two officers hand cuffed them, and they headed toward the escalator. The terminal was getting back to normal, many flights had been delayed, which meant the United Airlines system flights was going to be in chaos for a while.

The delays were due to misconnecting airlines, passengers, and flight crews around the system not connecting with one another. When one spoke of the hub gets disrupted and it's a large hub, then other segments of the routing structure will feel the impact. Flight crews get stranded or run out of duty time. And airplanes get out of sequence with their scheduled routes. It's chaos.

"I'm glad I don't work in crew scheduling or dispatch for United Airlines today," I told Stanton as we walked toward his office.

"I think you have the coolest office in the airport," I told him as he unlocked his door.

"Yep, kind of nice isn't it," he said, looking up to the famous theme restaurant that was directly above his office. "The airport manager was mighty kind to me when he gave me this space. It's in the center of the airport, I can easily walk to every terminal, I've got my own parking, and food right upstairs," he said. He slapped me on the back and laughed as I walked past him and into his office.

"Coffee?"

"Sure, I'd love some," I said.

"Let's call JJ so he can patch us into D.C. and get this over with," I said.

"There's the phone – dial away – I'll get the coffee going."

"Great, just like always! Make me do all the hard work," I whined as I dialed the operations centers number.

"Western-Pacific Operations Center, JJ speaking."

"Hey, JJ, it's Maggie, can you dial us into D.C. Our cell phones are dead. The situation at LAX is over and we, meaning Agent Stanton and I, need to report out on the incident. But before we do, has the media called yet?"

"Affirmative and I referred them to our public affairs desk in Northwest Mountain. "

"Great, thanks, good work, as always, JJ."

"Standby, Maggie, I'll get you connected to D.C. now."

Agent Stanton handed me a steaming cup of coffee and went and sat down in his chair behind his desk.

Behind him was a bookshelf full of modern model jet aircraft.

"I'm collecting one for each airline here at LAX," he said before I even opened my mouth.

"Well, they are impressive, but I think you'll need more shelves if you intend to collect all of them."

"Working on that now," he said with a grin.

The intercom crackled as the voices in D.C. came to life, demanding answers for events they were never really a part of.

After three cups of coffee without the benefit of donuts, we ended the call with a guarantee that the SITREP would be in D.C.'s hands before 0500 hours on Monday morning.

I looked over at Stanton and silently cursed, knowing that my beach time tomorrow, Sunday, with my kids just turned into a report writing party at the office – a party of one – and a party I didn't want to attend.

But when the Unabomber is involved, even if only in the film industry, the D.C. suits get unreasonable, meaning you work 24/7 until the paperwork is done.

"Hey, good to know it's not just me," Stanton said. "I get my butt chewed on a regular basis from D.C. for things I have no control over, but even with that said, this is, by far, the best job I have ever had."

With a sly grin and a smile, I chirped, "Me too."

"Listen, when the Unabomber threat happened and you were on your way out here from D.C. after working on the team that wrote the AVSEC (Aviation Security) contingency plan to counter the Unabomber threat, I got the call from D.C. And when I got the call, I hung up on Lee and Pete and came here to the airport as fast as my car would go. I think I hit 120 on the 405 freeway."

With my elbows on his desk, chin in my hands, I listened intently to what he had to do in response to the security directives that had been written in D.C. It was a team that I was on, in fact, a situation I had been called back to work for. I remember calling my neighbor to come watch my kids while I raced into the office. After pulling an all-nighter, racing back home, changing clothes, I got the kids off to school with lunches packed. Then I went back to work. It was insane. After being in D.C. for three years and never directly seeing how it impacted the field agents, I was glad to hear Lee's reaction to the Unabomber threat.

"I organized a response for the threat and stopped all mail from getting on airplanes until the next morning. Once the whole thing was organized and the Ops Center was put up in Terminal six, the security measures were in place and rock solid. That's what I did without the hand of God - I mean D.C. - telling me what to do. We're field agents. That's what we do."

"Yep, that's what we do."

"No one knows what we do, Maggie. They only see their cancelled or delayed flights, or that it takes longer to get through screening. But threats are real and we have to do something about them."

"We sure do. And now I'm going to get the heck out of here, find my kids, and then visit the nearest McDonalds so I can feed them while explaining why we won't have a beach day tomorrow."

"Been there, done that."

"Sure does suck. Yes indeed, crappy as hell on your family life, that's for sure. But I wouldn't trade this job or anything."

"Me either."

High fives and hugs later, I walked back to my car and headed for home. I picked Monica up at Emir's house and Mike at Bruno and Vinnie's. Their friends were the best--and more so their parents—for putting up with me and my crazy work schedule.

We opted for Taco Bell and called it a day around 11:00 P.M.

"Night, thank you, Lord," I said as I tucked myself into bed. It didn't take long for me to fall asleep.

Meanwhile, Agent Stanton was still awake and standing on his back patio, talking to his wife, Roberta, about the days' events.

"You know, sweetie, if Maggie didn't ask JJ to call me I wouldn't have known what happened until Monday when I went to work."

"Why? What happened?"

"The ops center in D.C. called my office number, not my cell number. You know how much good that did. You know me; most of the time I'm either out walking around the airport, or at a meeting, so calling my desk number was ludicrous. Especially on a Saturday!"

Roberta nodded.

"We've created positions to improve communications and continuity and the damn fools call the wrong number. Shit."

CHAPTER 3

Good Old Days

"Shucks, I don't want to get up!"

The Sandhill Crane alarm kept buzzing and buzzing in my ear no matter how many times I hit the snooze alarm. *But you've got to get up – staff meeting at 0630 – D.C. forgets we live on the West Coast. So get up.*

Agent Stanton had looked over the security summary draft for me yesterday. Together we made a few corrections. I hit the send button about 5:00 P.M.

At my desk, sipping my coffee, I listened to the mechanical hum of my computer, and the dull air conditioning drone on. I looked out my office window down at Century Blvd., as cars moved up and down the street in their haste to catch flights, pick someone up, or get to work on time.

I dialed into the conference call promptly as 6:30 A.M., announced that I was on the telecom and then immediately put my phone on mute. A few seconds later I heard Agent Stanton announce his presence, and I imagined he put his line on mute too.

The conference lasted about thirty minutes. Agent Stanton and I tag-teamed the briefing and by the time the two of us were done very few questions were left to ask by anyone in D.C., or by our management team at the regional office. Ed Smith, Tom Thomas, and Don

Harding were very pleased with the information that Lee and I had provided to them and to D.C. So once the formalities were out of the way, they let Lee and I do most of the talking. *That was always a good sign--flood them with a ton of information and you'll get left alone.* Today I wasn't in the mood to be second guessed.

After the conference call I tackled my in-box, reviewed about ten enforcement cases that needed my signature, and caught up on my email. It was a quiet and productive morning.

The only person that popped his head in the door was Special Agent Rich Gordon.

"Hey there, heard you had a long weekend. Need anything?"

"Nope, I'm good. Conference call with the R.O. and D.C. in a few minutes," I said.

"Later."

"Thanks," I hollered as he zipped around the corner and out of sight.

Agent Richard Gordon or Rich, as we all called him, was one of the agents hired by Tom Thomas a few months earlier. He didn't have a law enforcement background, he was a personal friend of Tom's, which potentially was a deadly combination for a new hire because he was a friend of management without law enforcement experience.

At first we all had reservations, but as we got to know Rich better, saw his work ethic and willingness to get the job done, everyone changed their minds. I saw him excel to the top of his class time and time again at the FAA training facility in Oklahoma City. The more I saw, the more I liked.

He was going to be one of our best.

Rich's office was next door to mine, which allowed the two of us to talk more since we walked past one another's office frequently. He was older than the rest of the team, closer to my age, kids, a wife, and a fun personality. I don't think he thought one thing about not being liked; he smiled, greeted everyone by their first name, and worked his butt off.

In late summer, August 9th to be exact, the Secretary of Transportation had directed a reasonable and prudent increase in security measures by airports and air carriers in the United States. That mandate gave the FAA authority to hire more special agents to inspect both airports and airlines; the AVSEC security measures required not only permanent changes, but some emergency security requirements, all based on assessments from law enforcement and intelligence agencies. Threats from Ramzi Yousef, the Unabomber, were changing the face of aviation security.

Without a doubt additional staffing was a welcome relief for every office in the country. My only personal complaint was it seemed that D.C. always got more staffing than the field. And the bulk of the security work was done at the field level, not in headquarters.

And Rich wasn't a FAM – no nickname – we all called him Rich.

Me on the other hand – I had a nickname – I was called Mad Dog. Everyone in FAM school gets a nickname – that is, if you're liked. I earned mine one day during an early training run with my team out in Marana, Arizona. We had to run a mile and a half in under twelve minutes. I always trailed the pack with a smile on my face – I was the dreamer in the group – never imagining that running fast might be vital to my career. Running fast was not in my vocabulary – until then! On qualification day to become an air marshal I ran really fast, imagining that I was being chased by bad guys. I managed to outrun everyone as if I was a madwoman on steroids. I gave it my all that day – and "Mad Dog" Stewart emerged that day like a hungry coyote howling for food, and knowing she might have to fight to keep it.

Now, years later, desk bound most of the time, I still kept in shape. In fact, I would be running my first marathon a few weeks. I'd been seriously training for the Palos Verdes Marathon and I was just about ready to go. My longest run, weekend before last, was 22 miles. Next weekend I was running 24 miles, then two weeks after that I'd race.

The FAM program had changed significantly since I'd gotten out of the program. The training facility had been moved from Marana, Arizona to an FAA facility in Atlantic City, New Jersey. It was a positive step forward, the facility was very modern, and an aircraft was used for tactical training.

But other steps backward included making significant changes to the firearms qualifications course, and to the physical fitness qualification standards. Male and female were required to meet identical physical fitness requirements. Only one existing female air marshal passed the new qualifications. Needless to say, several of the women that didn't pass filed EEO complaints against management. I didn't blame them for filing complaints. To me, being able to do the same amount of push-ups and sit-ups as a man was out of balance. Now shooting as accurately is an absolute and should require equal abilities. But push-ups and sit-ups, I didn't agree at all.

Another change was that each team being deployed would travel to D.C. several days before their scheduled mission and re-qualify. If they didn't pass they would be replaced with another team member and sent home.

It was a very different program from when I flew. The cadre was still small in numbers but growing in proficiency, expertise, and reputation under the leadership of Greg McDillon, the Director of the Federal Air Marshal program. All FAMs were still volunteers; when they weren't flying they worked as FAA Inspectors based at various field offices throughout the country.

Most of the FAMs I had flown with were no longer in the program. Many of us, (Lee Stanton, Big Earl, Georgia H., Dan M., Rusty P., Mike G., and Paul G.) had moved into various supervisory or management positions in the FAA either in the U.S. or at one of our overseas locations. We were spread out around the world now, tackling diplomatic affairs in foreign countries, working with airports and airlines here at home to comply with the ever-changing code of federal regulations, or managing agents and support staff. We were all now a part of the bureaucratic machinery, yet we worked tirelessly to protect airline crews and the passengers they served…we served. Like an enormous puzzle, we each were a piece which needed the rest of the pieces to be complete.

I believed that being a FAM was a real building block for moving into other positions of authority within FAA security. We FAMs were a tight network of highly skilled individuals, we worked efficiently and competently protecting the public. We trusted each other and the public trusted us.

CHAPTER **4**

Going the Distance

I was ready! Standing tall and proud to be an American, I was filled with a jittery energy that I was anxious to release! Hearing our national anthem, then the sound of the gun, I shouted my cheers along with hundreds of other runners as we all began our quest to reach the finish line.

It was a perfect May morning. Fog dripped, rolled, and oozed its way along the Palos Verdes cliffs. The ocean, hundreds of feet below, slapped and crashed into the shore greeting us one by one as we passed the wooded barrier separating us. Gulls and pelicans flew past in groups or alone in search of breakfast.

Remember your pace, Maggie, remember your training. Go the distance, and smile.

I had been training three months for this morning. It was my first official foot race. I paid an entry fee to run 26.2 miles and I was excited as heck. It all began after I saw Oprah Winfrey run a marathon. So here I was, many months later, fully prepared and ready to go.

I trained alone. I ran alone. Alone--just as I had done in my initial training, and subsequent recurrent training runs to become a FAM and then to stay a FAM.

I had always loved to run. I love its mechanical rote system and rhythm. Running is primordial, was essential for survival to catch food, escape enemies, for our early transportation--and is now for most a sport. For me, it's still essential for my sanity, my survival. *Mad Dog, lone dog, I loved to run.*

Like the solitude of the desert skies early in the morning, I found solace in the morning sky here at the beach. Swathes of red and gray greeted me as the sun rose. The foggy overcast made it even quieter except for the thundering feet of the runners that paced beside me, or that raced by me. No one behind me now. *Too early to rush, Maggie,* I muttered to myself.

Earlier that morning I'd hugged both of my kids as they dreamily slept tucked warm, safely in their beds and headed downstairs. I let Sandee, our dog, out and waited, tapping my fingers on the kitchen counter top, for my everything-on-it bagel to toast. But no cream cheese this morning, just a plain bagel.

"Kind of boring, isn't it?" I said to the dog as I let her back in the house. "And by the way, I'm only having one cup of coffee this morning."

She wagged her tail, opened her mouth to show her purple Chow tongue, clearly showing interest, but I knew she really only wanted her breakfast too.

"Okay, okay, I'm getting it now," I said, patting her blonde head.

Passing the five mile marker, I grabbed another cup of Gatorade and continued my self-imposed pace.

This older man came up alongside me and he nodded his head as a 'good morning' gesture. He wasn't wearing a shirt and, I have to admit, I'd never seen a man with so much hair on his chest and his back. It was kind of gross, but runners can be kind of gross. At least he wasn't spitting, making exaggerated noises of excruciating pain, or trying to cut me off.

Then he smiled. An old man smile, every piece of skin on his face wrinkled up into a flabby but very happy smile. "Hello."

"Hi, how's it going?"

"So far, so good. Run this before?"

"Nope, this is my first official race ever. In fact, it's my first marathon," I said as we wound our way along Palos Verdes Drive South toward the halfway point at Wayfarers' Chapel.

"Good on you," he said. "Let me give you a tip. When you get near a corner, or a curve, run the apex, or the inside of the curve, so you make the turn as efficiently as possible. You'll save hundreds of steps during a marathon."

"Really?"

"Really," he commented.

"Thanks."

And away he went. Moving forward, steadily, quietly, his hairy back glistening in the morning sunlight.

I held back, continuing on at my training pace. I was comfortable, happy, and confident. As I passed Wayfarers' Chapel, one fourth of the way to the finish I saw the rolling, gentle hills of PV still ahead of me. The steepest part of the course, 25th Street, was behind me, and the next set of hills were small grades rolling downhill as if trying to finally meet the sea. When I saw the rolling downhill, I knew the up-hill would be on the way back, around the 20-mile mark. Killer hills at the end!

Five hours and seventeen minutes later I crossed the finish line. Dripping with perspiration, I could taste the salt as I licked my lips, my legs felt like lead, my feet hurt, but I was still smiling. I beamed as the volunteer handed me my finishers' medal.

"Thanks."

"Good job," the volunteer replied.

I had run my first marathon. The exhilaration was intoxicating as I happily hobbled the half mile back to my Jeep.

"Shucks," I said. Glancing down at my left tennis shoe I saw a blood stain, so I knew my toes probably looked like they felt. But in my mind, I was already planning my next race.

No pain, no gain. I walked up the steep hill toward the San Pedro Friendship Bell parking lot. *I would definitely be running this again next year.*

Unlocking my car, I grabbed the gallon of water, towel, and

sandals I had put in the back of the Jeep. I sat down, untied my shoes, and examined my sore and slightly swollen big toe. I washed and dried my feet, before putting on my flip-flops. I stretched a few more times before I finally got in the car for the easy twenty-five minute ride home.

I wasn't especially sore when I got up for work the next morning, which was Monday, but on Tuesday I could barely walk down a single flight of stairs. And my left big toe required the use of sandals – one big toe nail was clearly going to be lost.

The glory of being a runner. I poured my first cup of coffee.

I was hooked!

CHAPTER 5

Finally Got Caught

"They caught him, Maggie," Agent Stanton said, walking into my office.

"Who"?

"Ted Kaczynski, the Unabomber."

"Really? Where? When? How?" I asked in one breath.

"FBI and local law enforcement caught him just outside of Lincoln, Montana. He had a mountain cabin and a family member tipped the FBI off that he might be responsible for the mail bomb killings."

"That's great news, Stanton."

"Seems like a pretty solid lead too. Neighbors at the saw mill near the cabin also ID him as Theodore (Ted) Kaczynski. Said Ted kept to himself most of the time, didn't own a car, lived like a hermit, and he occasionally rode his bicycle into the town to get groceries."

"I know the FBI has been looking for the Unabomber for years now. Personally, I didn't even know about him until he moved into the aviation arena with the mail bombs. Once he impacted the FAA, and us, I learned a whole lot more about him. He's a bad guy, without a doubt, if it turns out to be him."

"Looks like this threat might be winding down, now that he's been captured," Stanton said.

"When did he start mailing bombs? Was it '78 or '79?"

"The report I saw this morning said 1978. He was mailing bombs targeting universities and then airlines. First he hit the University of Illinois at Chicago, then a return package from the postal service exploded at Northwestern University. This guy is a real piece of work."

"I wonder if any of our security measures pertaining to this threat will be modified."

"Probably a few, but you know the FAA. Once policies and directives get implemented, it's hard to convince anyone to change them if they won't impact us immediately. And, if by chance they do get changed, I think it will take a while."

"Here's the latest from CNN," I said. "The news is reporting that this guy mailed a least fifteen bombs, most of them packages, injured twenty-three people, and killed three people."

"Yep, and remember his manifesto. The DOJ published it because the Unabomber threatened to blow more people up if the New York Times and the Washington Post didn't publish it."

"I hope the guy never sees daylight again."

"I do too."

When my telephone rang Agent Stanton and I knew it was probably the regional office calling.

"Office of Civil Aviation Security, Agent Stewart," I said.

"Maggie, its JJ. Tom needs you to dial into a national telecom. Here's the number."

"I'll dial in now. Thanks JJ."

"Want to stick around and listen in," I asked Stanton.

"Sure."

Seconds after the telecom began, Agent Stanton's cell phone rang.

"Thank God for the mute button," I said to him with a smile. "Bet D.C. is looking for you now."

"About time," he said as he got up from the chair, answered his phone, and waved goodbye simultaneously.

. . .

Turning off Dufour Avenue and into my driveway, I was glad to have a few rays of sunlight left because I desperately needed to go for a short run before I started dinner.

"Hi Mom," Monica said as I walked in the door. She was sitting in the oversized green leather chair watching TV. Our chow/lab mix dog was curled up at her feet.

"Hey, Bean. How'd your day go? Do you have any homework?"

"Good and nope."

"Great. Where's your brother?"

"He's at Spencer's. He said he'd be home by dark."

As I climbed the stairs, I shouted, "Perfect. I'm going for a short run and then I'll make dinner."

"Okay, Mom."

. . .

Forty-five minutes later I was making beef tacos for dinner, sipping on a glass of Chardonnay, watching CNN discuss the entire morbid life history of Ted Kaczynski, showing news clips of him handcuffed, being taken into custody at the FBI offices in downtown Helena. He was 5′9″ and appeared relatively young, but he stooped as he walked, his scraggly hair flopping in the light spring breeze.

An end to an era, I said to myself while stirring the taco seasoning into the beef.

"Spring break is about ten days away," I said to the kids during dinner. "Are you still okay with going to Emir's house, while Mike and I go camping with his Boy Scout troop, Monica?"

She nodded, her mouth full. She was more than ready to escape to her best friend's house, leaving behind both her brother and me.

"Okay, last chance. I'll call Emir's tomorrow, Mom, and confirm it's okay one last time too."

"K, Mom."

"Let's get these dishes picked up. You wash, Monica, and you put them in the dishwasher, Michael. I'll let the dog out. Deal?"

"Deal," they said at the same time.

Finally the house was quiet. The kids were fast asleep and the neighbors' dog had finally been taken in for the night, so her high pitched yapping, at every leaf that moved with the wind, had finally stopped.

Sure hasn't done any good to talk to them about their dog has it, Maggie? I muttered as I climbed the stairs to my bedroom.

I peeked inside the kids' bedrooms and smiled at their relaxed positions, gentle breathing, and blissful faces while they slept. My heart filled with joy and love when I saw them safely in their beds.

. . .

Two weeks later Mike, fifteen other boys, and five adults were packing into various vans, trucks and one RV for the three hundred mile drive to Zion National Park in Utah. I had never been there, much less on a camping trip with sixteen Boy Scouts and troop leaders.

A few months earlier, my son had come home announcing that their troop needed another adult leader for their upcoming 50-mile-hike camping trip and he volunteered me. When Dan, the scout leader, called to discuss the trip with me I was really excited about going to a national park, but not certain if I could tent camp for ten days with a bunch of 15-year-old scouts. And the trip entailed a 50-mile hike for a merit badge, which was why I was asked. Not too many parents had volunteered to go along. My son, Mike, knew I ran a lot, and long distances, so he naively assumed I could hike with a backpack too.

Once I committed, I started walking in the neighborhood with a day pack full of canned goods and water so I'd get used to carrying a 40-pound backpack. I actually got pretty good at it too!

Piece of cake, I've got this, Maggie.

Driving north on Interstate 15, passing Las Vegas, North Las Vegas, and into the barren desert I thought back to my Marana training days. When I signed on to become a federal air marshal it was unknown territory for me back then too. When I began basic training I was a bundle of varying emotions – confidence, nervousness but I ultimately excelled. And I would excel now too.

"My oh my, look at that, Mike," I said, pointing out the front window as we drove into the Virgin River Gorge, beginning our fairly steep ascent uphill into the twisty, winding, windswept road that was taking us toward the city of St. George, Utah and then on to Zion. Mike looked out the windshield of the passenger seat as his friends, Bobby and Bruno, looked out the side back seat windows.

The black, brown, red, orange, and tan rocks were massive. Their beauty and majesty was raw, eloquent, and breathtaking. For a few brief seconds the boys were speechless. I drove as slowly as I could, allowing as much time as possible to take in the rough beauty that was unfolding before our eyes.

Passing through the gorge, we flattened out to the desert floor once again. But now we could see thunderstorms building far off in the distant mountains, buffeting up against their towering walls of red, brown, and black. It was a stunning sight.

Several hours later, after picking out our campsite, we began setting up tents, and got ready to settle in for the evening. Being one of the only ladies on the trip (two other mothers were along, but were camping in an RV), I set my tent up on the edge of the campsite, beneath a tree where I could see all of the kids' tents. A stream that ran alongside the campsite looked mighty inviting for a cool swim. I knew we'd only be camping there two nights because night three and four would be spent in The Narrows, an adventure waiting to unfold.

The Boy Scout troop was from the local Mormon Church; everyone on the trip was Mormon except Mike. Mike joined this scout group because his two best friends were Mormon. On Sunday we were supposed to stay in camp and rest.

Walking over to the scout leader, Tommy, I said, "I think we all should go and get a bath."

"Why?" Tommy asked.

"We got here late yesterday. We sat in hot cars all day. We got camp set-up just before dark. And it's roasting hot today," I continued. "I think we all need to go upstream and get cleaned up."

He looked at me with a puzzled look. But then he slowly began to understand what I was hinting at.

"I think that's an excellent idea. I think you might be onto something."

I winked, nodded, and gave a conspiratorial look that sealed the deal.

"Okay. Come on guys, let's go, get your towels," he commanded all of the boys. "We need to bathe."

"What's going on, Mom?" Mike asked.

"These kids don't do anything on Sunday except rest and praise God. I love God too – but we all are roasting. I suggested we continue to praise God along with getting cooler and clean. The only place here to clean up is to go upstream and soak. So we're off to soak."

Back at the campground several hours later I was satisfied that we were all sufficiently clean.

Shortly after dinner we held a group meeting to make sure everyone had their gear and supplies ready for the hike through The Narrows that we'd all be embarking on the following morning.

"We're going to hike half The Narrows tomorrow, camp, and hike out the following morning. The hike is sixteen miles and most of it involves hiking through the river so you'll get wet. Your gear can get wet if you don't pack it properly, and you need to watch out for each other. So don't be speed freaks."

Once Tommy was satisfied everything was in order we all headed for our tents in an attempt to sleep.

"Are you excited, Mike?" I asked my son before he headed off to his tent.

"I sure am, Mom. You?"

"I'm ready. This is going to be a blast."

"For sure. Night. Love you."

"Love you too, Mikey. Thanks for bringing me along."

. . .

"Let's go – time to move out, kids," Tommy ordered everyone. "Grab your backpacks and pile into the RV."

Riding along Highway 9 we drove toward Chamberlin Ranch, which would be the drop off point to hike the narrows. During the forty-five minute ride the air was filled with the chatter of excited boys.

"Here we are, boys," Tommy said as the RV stopped at an iron gate that said 'No Trespassing.' As if reading our minds Tommy told us it was okay to pass through this area as long as we had a back country pass to hike The Narrows.

With waves and huge smiles we waved as Fred and Mary drove away, bouncing and jerking along in their RV as they began their journey back to Watchman Campground.

The first few miles of our hike were through farmland. We stayed close to the river's edge in an open flat area. As we neared the Narrows the sandstone sides of the canyon walls began displaying the gallery of sculptured rock that was created from the running water of the river and the wind sweeping through the valley.

Continuing downriver we walked into a place of pure peace and refuge. It was magnificent. My camera, tucked away in several plastic bags, was easy to reach since I had packed it in the top zipper pouch of my backpack. The vividly colored cliffs towering above me mandated that I snap one picture after another.

"This place is breathtaking, Tommy."

"Sure is, that's why we come here every year to hike. And we grew up in St. George, so it's always good to come home."

"I'm not sure I'd ever want to move away if I grew up with this in my backyard."

"Not much work out here. I had to move to find work."

The further downriver we hiked, the higher the canyon walls closed in on us and at one point when we stretched out our arms we could nearly touch the walls to our left and right.

"Spectacular," I said.

We reached our campsite around 5:00 P.M., cooked noodles on

small camp stoves, and called it a day. I didn't carry a tent or a canopy so I snuggled into my sleeping bag with the stars as my night light.

I listened to the river water racing past, the wind whistling through the canyon, rustling the leaves on the small trees. I watched in awe as the stars moved across the sky as the earth turned and turned. It was magical, marvelous, and spiritual.

However, as we gathered together the next morning to begin the second day of our hiking, it wasn't as magical. It was freezing cold. Everything was damp and wet.

"Today we'll be hiking through the deepest parts of the river," Tommy said. "You will need to carry your gear over your head in some places. And keep together. We'll meet at the beginning of the Zion River Walk. When you get there, stop, and wait for the rest of us."

"Got it," one of boys said enthusiastically.

"Hold up! I'm not finished! Wait at the river walk because we're going to hike the last mile out together. Understood?"

Everyone nodded their heads, as they looked downstream. The boys were anxious to get going.

"Okay, let's go."

"Yikes, the water is freezing this morning," I exclaimed, stuffing a granola bar into my mouth, followed by a gulp of water.

No coffee girl. Mormons don't drink coffee. Drat!

"My toes are numb, my fingers are numb, and I think my brain is numb," I said as I slowly shuffled my shoes along the smooth, well rounded river rocks, feeling the current of the river swirl around my ankles. "It's so beautiful here that I can't comprehend it. My brain feels numb, but I know it's not."

Whoa, saved by my walking stick. I stepped up, over, and slipped on a wet rock. Crashing down on one knee, I broke two nails, skinned my shin, but somehow managed to keep my backpack dry.

Mike began wading toward me shouting, "Are you okay, Mom?"

Relatively unscathed I hollered back, "I'm fine, keep going, son. I'll see you at the bottom."

"Okay." And he was off like a shot with the rest of his friends.

As for me, I was exhausted, cold, but having the time of my life. The red rocks had seeped into my soul like the river water had seeped into the soles of my shoes. Zion was magical. It was heaven on earth and I was happy beyond words. I knew I would return here again and again.

Hours later, even more exhausted, I began seeing hikers traveling up the river. I knew I was close to the end because a lot of day hikers walk up the river, passing by with waves, smiles, and laughter. Their facial expressions are alive and lit with the excitement of seeing such a glorious place.

As I stepped from the river onto the cement path called The River Walk, I saw several boys from the troop, some standing, others sitting, and others splashing and playing in the shallow water.

Finally, the troop was all together, and we hiked the last mile out as a group. Everyone was exhausted, wet, dirty, and very proud of their accomplishments. The ride on the parks transportation system back to our campground was filled with stories, laughter, and tales of bravado. Like fishing, camping always has room for tall tales!

. . .

The alarm went off at 5:00 A.M. the following Monday morning. I had been dreaming about red rocks, windswept canyons, gorgeous sandstone, and rivers. It was a dream I didn't want to leave.

CHAPTER 6

A Turbulent Year

An hour and fifteen minutes later I was at the office watching CNN discuss the entire morbid life history of Ted Kaczynski, again, while replaying news clips of him handcuffed, and being taken into custody at the FBI offices in downtown Helena. It seemed being gone a week had only temporarily blotted out my memory of bad guys because in reality the world was full of them.

The summer passed, slipping into fall, and then lazily to winter. As the summer winds became cool winter breezes, the aviation security community changed wind direction too.

"Maggie's on," I said in response to Tom's roll call request.

"Cal's on," said my counterpart, Cal Yates, manager at the San Francisco Civil Aviation Security Field Office.

Once roll call for the five offices: Los Angeles, San Francisco, Honolulu, Las Vegas, and Phoenix, was complete Tom Thomas, the deputy division manager for the Western-Pacific Region began, "Good morning, everyone. This telecom should be brief. I wanted to let each of you know what's going on at the San Francisco Airport this afternoon."

Clearing his throat, Tom continued, "Headquarters has selected San Francisco Airport as a demonstration site for the first explosive detection system demonstrations."

I heard Cal Yates say, "Hear, hear," and clapping in the background.

"What I want each manager to do, including you Art in Hawaii, is to travel to San Francisco in the next few months and watch the demonstration. FAA Security's goal is to eventually have these explosive detection systems (EDS) at every Category X and some of the larger Category one airports by the end of next year. Once again the Western-Pacific Region is on the cutting edge of technology. Are there any questions?"

The entire telecom lasted a little over an hour. After discussing the EDS, necessary, but not nearly as interesting topics were discussed, including staffing, overtime, case-load distribution, EIR returns from AWP-720 for content error or additional clarification. Finally, Don Harding agreed to set up an information meeting between legal and the agents to discuss how to make cases stronger for legal.

"We work so hard during our inspections, and when we find violations, write a case, and submit it to legal, it is really, really frustrating when it gets closed with a 'No Action'," I said.

"The agents are beginning to think, why bother? The case is just going to get closed by legal or mitigated so far down from the original civil penalty, that what's the point?" Doug from the Las Vegas office said.

"I hear you," Don said. "I'll set up a meeting with legal."

When Stanton called, I began telling him about the EDS testing going on in San Francisco.

"Just got off a telecom too, Maggie. Pete Flint briefed all of the FSMs about the EDS equipment in San Francisco. I'm flying up the first of next week to check it out. Pete is flying out from D.C. Want to tag along?"

"No, I'm going to head up with Doug and Big Earl this Friday. Tom said to go ASAP, so we're going ASAP."

"Okay, I'm heading over to American Airlines to look at some items they confiscated from checked luggage. I'll call you later."

"Let me know if it's anything interesting. Bye."

Several hours later when I picked up the ringing telephone I heard Agent Stanton laughing.

"Well, there's a sound I don't hear too often. What's so funny?"

"You are not going to believe what American had to show me at the cargo facility, Maggie."

"What?"

"A man wanted to check his tool bag along with chain saw in at the ticket counter this morning. The guy couldn't comprehend that the gasoline in the tank and a chain saw that worked might cause a problem on an airplane once airborne!"

"I hear you. You've got to love the traveling public."

"The guy then refused to take it back to his car when the ticket agent gave him that option. American refused to check it in as luggage. So the guy only checked his tool kit, and told the agent he'd get his chain saw when he got back. He'd be late for his flight if he went back to his car!"

"Did they tell him it won't be there when he gets back?"

"Don't know."

"We need more oversight and regulations regarding checked baggage, that's for sure."

"We sure do, and speaking of regulations, did you see the draft Unescorted Access Privilege Rule that came out earlier this week?"

"I have it here on my desk. I'll put a team together here in the office to read the entire proposed regulation and see how much work it's going to be for the agents."

"Good idea, Maggie. I think it's going to be a ton of work. Now any employee that wants to be in a restricted area with unescorted access is going to need an employment history check first. That's going to be a huge and expensive undertaking for the airports to implement. And it's going to be labor intensive for us to make sure that the checks are actually being done, not just a paper exercise."

"But we'll get it done, Maggie. That's what we do. I'll talk to you later."

"Yes, we will. Bye."

. . .

I was halfway through my 10-mile run when my cell phone rang. "Hello."

"Mom, Mom, Sandee's got Bob in her mouth and she's running around the front yard," Monica screamed into the phone.

"Great. Did you try to get her to drop Bob?"

"Yes, but she won't listen to me."

"I'm on my way back, but it's going to take me close to an hour to get there. Get the dog in the house if you can. How'd she get Bob, anyway?"

"Mike left his bedroom door open."

"Well, that will do it. See you as fast as I can get there."

True to form, when I got home, no one had listened to a word I'd said.

Sandee was running around the front yard with Bob, our box turtle, stuck firmly in her mouth. Monica and Mike were chasing the dog, their arms flailing wildly, and screaming for the dog to stop.

Pure chaos. I grabbed her by the collar, and said, "Drop it. Drop Bob now, dog."

The dog didn't listen either. I stuck my fingers into her mouth, prying open her purple blackish chow jaws, as I continued to yell. "Drop Bob. Drop Bob now." With grit on my part, coupled with a lot of yelling, Sandee finally let go of Bob.

Plopping to the ground, Bob immediately buried his head inside his shell. He had puncture wounds along the outer edge of his shell but he was still alive. I knew we needed to get to a veterinarian.

Racing inside, I put Bob in the kitchen sink, got out the telephone book and looked for a veterinarian to call. It was 2:00 P.M. on a Saturday so I wasn't sure who would be open. I had to find a reptile veterinarian so the list shrunk down to one.

When I called they were still open and suggested that I bring Bob in right away. Looking down at Bob in the sink, he was definitely not going to come out of his shell anytime soon.

"Mike, put the dog in the backyard. Monica, get a shoe box out of the garage. Let's get Bob to the vet."

Two and a half hours later, and with a $600 dollar charge on my VISA credit card, Bob was wrapped in purple gauze which had to be changed once a week, at the vet's, for three weeks in a row!

I would have put the darn turtle to sleep if I didn't have two kids bawling their eyes out at the vet's office. I began cooking dinner. *What a mess, but I just couldn't do it!*

The following morning, Mother's Day, I was greeted in bed by two very excited children who had made pancakes and coffee for me. They presented me with a handmade card signed by both of them, a paw print from the dog, and a scratch mark from the turtle.

"I love you guys," I said, hugging them. "This is the best Mother's Day ever."

Then the telephone rang…

"Maggie, its JJ. I've got Tom on the line."

"Uh oh."

"Maggie, Tom here. There's been a crash out of Miami. Washington, D.C. Operations Center just called. I don't have very many details yet. Images are just starting to come up on CNN now."

"What kind of flight; passenger or cargo? Do we know yet?" I asked.

"Passenger, and it crashed in the Everglades after leaving Miami International on its way to Atlanta, Georgia. I'm giving you a heads-up to be on standby for the rest of the afternoon in case we need to deploy agents to our airports."

"Roger that, Tom."

"I'll talk to you later." The line disconnected.

"Thanks, JJ."

"Any time, Maggie. Let me know if you need anything."

I walked into the family room, turned on the TV, and stood watching CNN. The news reports were beginning to flood in. They even had eyewitnesses who said they watched as the plane rolled onto its side and plowed, nose first, into the Everglades, just a few miles west of Miami.

Later a group of fisherman who saw the crash were interviewed, saying they saw the plane make a steep right bank, and then its nose went straight down, plummeting into the swamp water. Then an explosion, a shock wave, and a massive geyser of water appeared.

"It was horrible," the stunned fisherman said to the news reporter, shaking his head as if trying to shake away the terrible memory.

Late into the evening CNN was reporting that the passenger DC-9 was owned and operated by ValuJet. ValuJet 592 had crashed into the Everglades and it was feared that all 110 people on board had been killed.

I drank my third glass of wine, went upstairs, stared into my kids' rooms, and went to bed.

At 4:00 A.M., I was wide awake, staring at the ceiling, listening to the wind blow through the bottle brush tree that was just outside my bedroom window.

"Give it up, Maggie," I murmured. "Get up. This is useless." I put on my robe, walked downstairs, turned on the coffee pot, then the TV and waited to see the latest information on the doomed jetliner.

CNN reported that at 2:13 P.M. flight 592 had disappeared from radar. The flight crew and all of the passengers had died instantly when the airplane traveling at 507 MPH slammed into the Everglades within less than ten seconds. The passengers were in pieces now, mingled in with other debris, saw grass, alligators, and water. Scattered remains littered the swamp and the initial examination of the crash site suggested there was some kind of fire onboard.

Arriving at the office at 5:15 A.M. I knew I'd be the first one there, and today I was happy to have a few moments of solitude before starting my day. I rode the elevator to the fifth floor, punched in the security code to the main office door, and headed down the hall to make coffee. As I looked out the windows I could see the orange, red, and gray colors begin to light the sky as dawn unveiled itself on Los Angeles.

. . .

Several months later most of ValuJet's parts, pieces, and remaining body parts had been retrieved, and the investigation into the cause was underway.

We had increased security in every area; increased checkpoint testing, observed how the airports performed employment background checks for any employee that wanted an airport identification that gave them unrestricted and unescorted access around the airport. We enhanced and increased the number of scheduled inspections for every airport the FAA regulated. Unlimited overtime was approved because we didn't have the authorization to hire and train any additional special agents.

And then it happened again!

The telephone rang…

"Maggie, its JJ. I've got Tom on the line."

"Okay."

"Maggie, Tom here. There's been a crash out of New York. Washington, D.C. Operations Center just called. I don't have very many details yet. Images are just starting to come up on CNN now."

"No – not again, Tom. What kind of flight; passenger or cargo? Do we know yet?" I asked.

"Passenger and it crashed in the Atlantic Ocean from John F. Kennedy Airport on its way to Rome. You'll probably have to come back to the office tonight."

"Roger that, Tom."

"I'll talk to you later." The line disconnected.

"Thanks, JJ."

"Any time, Maggie. Let me know if you need anything."

As soon as I walked in my door at home I needed to lace up my running shoes and go for a five-mile run. I'd cook when I got back. Mike was at Toni's house. Monica was watching TV.

"I'm off for a quick run, Monica. Love you," I said as I headed out the door.

"Okay, Mom."

I raced toward the beach, running with all my might. I ran fast down Manhattan Beach Boulevard., up and over the gentle rolling hills toward the ocean. As I pushed my feet forward I managed to miss most of the traffic lights. I ran to the end of the Manhattan Beach Pier before I turned back to begin the two mile run back toward home.

I raced as if I was running for my life. I was frustrated, sad, and angry all at the same time. We were dealing with aviation tragedies that did not yet have a story ending; was it mechanical failure, pilot error, terrorists…?" Why did ValuJet crash and now TWA?

. . .

Days turned into weeks and weeks into months. One hundred and ten souls perished on ValuJet 592 back in May and then 230 died on TWA 800.

In September the White House Commission on Aviation Safety and Security distributed a final report that approved additional funding for FAA security staffing. This report outlined expanded security program regulations and equipment to be used in the dangerous goods and air cargo security program.

"We're in for a lot of changes."

"About darn time," Stanton said. "I've been talking to my boss in D.C. for years now about cargo security. These changes are excellent and long overdue."

"More agents are at the training academy in Oklahoma City too. They have been hired specifically for inspecting cargo and dangerous goods. I hear Bill Willis is heading the cargo security program. He is relentless in making sure the toughest security measures are adhered to. We're lucky to have him in D.C."

"What a year, Maggie. What a year."

CHAPTER 7

An Emerging Threat

"Hi, Maggie. It's Chief Linden."

"Hey, how are you?"

"Good thanks. I'd like to set up an appointment to meet with you as soon as you're available. We've been getting some unusual activity out here with lasers and I think you'll be interested."

"I'll come out tomorrow morning. How's ten A.M.?"

After I hung up I wrote the appointment time in my planner.

Still using paper. One of these days I'd switch, but not today.

Captain Linden is the Chief Safety Officer at Ontario Airport. He is the captain for the fire department and also with law enforcement and protection services for both Ontario and Los Angeles. The responsibilities of fire and police were usually separate at airports but in this case they were combined. Needless to say, Lindsay was a very busy man.

The following morning I parked my government car by the maintenance shed near the main terminal entrance and slowly made my way to the terminal. I was carrying a briefcase that held an inert hand grenade so I could do some checkpoint testing before my 10:00 meeting.

New face at the checkpoint so let's see what happens.

The line to the checkpoint was congested before the inspection point so I felt confident that I wasn't seen. When that happens, the screeners usually get wise to the FAA tests. But today I knew that I'd get my bag through without anyone initially realizing that a test was taking place.

You'd think after all these years that I wouldn't be nervous anymore. But before starting an investigation or test, there was a familiar fluttering of my heart, a feeling of risk, an awareness that my actions were going to create a reaction. I hoped the reaction was of recognition of the device, not letting it pass.

I placed my briefcase on the belt and moved at a snail's pace forward as the briefcase slowly moved along the back rubber belt toward the mouth of the x-ray machine. I made a habit of waiting until all of my carry-on items were well into the machine before passing through the walk-through metal detector. It eased my mind about anyone stealing anything, and in this case it ensured that my briefcase had already been screened.

It was important that it be screened. Once the briefcase entered the machine I walked over and went through the metal detector. "Good morning," I said as I showed them my credentials.

"Good morning," the screener said in return as I reached over and picked up my briefcase.

With the briefcase in one hand and my FAA Special Agent credentials in the other I walked over to the podium where the screening manager and law enforcement were located.

"Good morning. I just passed through lane three at your checkpoint and I have a grenade in my briefcase that the screener did not detect," I said to the manager.

"Oh no," said the manager.

As I was writing down the time, location, and names of the screener and manager I advised them, "You know this is a violation of FAR 108.9, Screening of Passengers and Property, yes?"

"Unfortunately, yes. I'll pull the screener right now from the checkpoint," the manager advised.

"That's a good start. I'm going to advise the station manager that there was a checkpoint failure here."

On my way to meet Captain Linden I stopped at the American Airlines ticket counter and spoke to one of the ticket agents.

"Hi, I'm Maggie Stewart with FAA Security. Would you please give your manager my business card? I need him to call me ASAP please. I ran a test at the checkpoint a few minutes ago and the screener failed."

"Okay, I'll let him know."

"Thanks." I turned away and headed for my 10:00 meeting.

Arriving a few minutes late, I apologized and explained my tardiness.

"Maggie, this is Robert Bunk, he's a professor at U.C. Claremont specializing in military combat studies."

I was curious as to why the captain invited a 'civilian' to our meeting, but in reality the captain was a civilian too. I had an enormous amount of respect for Captain Linden, so after shaking hands and pouring myself a cup of coffee, I sat down at the conference table with them.

It didn't take me long to understand why Bunk was invited to this meeting.

"He's an expert in the transition from medieval to modern weaponry, legacy systems, and conventional firearms. He studies emerging threats too. And I think we've got an emerging threat on our hands, Maggie."

"Really, what's going on?"

"About a month ago, on approach here, a United Airlines pilot reported that the cockpit of his airplane was illuminated by what appeared to be a laser beam. "

Sitting up a little straighter, my interest was definitely piqued.

"We didn't report it because originally we thought it was an anomaly, a one-time occurrence, but it happened again, two more times, to another commercial airline and then to an Ontario police helicopter."

I was listening and writing notes at the same time. "Any injuries?"

"So far there haven't been any injuries."

"The mechanics of visual disruption can only be described in terms of the effect produced when the eye interacts with the light, specifically changes in light hitting the eye. In commercial aircraft, with fewer windows, less light can enter, but in a helicopter, it is very easy to illuminate the entire cockpit. There lies the potential to temporarily blind the pilot."

"I'm with you, I understand," I said. "Glare is a common expectation, but an intense light source, like a laser, is a real problem."

I understood because before I joined the FAA I was a student pilot, flying around in a Cessna 150, and my ex-husband was a pilot, I understood the importance of sight, both during the day and at night.

"Yes, the sudden illumination and resulting glare of collimated laser beam radiation, amplified by reflection and refraction in the cockpit is a real danger," Bunk said.

"And unfortunately a reflected or refracted laser radiation hitting a cockpit canopy can produce flash blindness," said Captain Linden.

"I had no idea. I think our folks will definitely be interested in this, along with air traffic and flight standards," I said.

"Good, I'm convinced that this is an emerging threat," stated Captain Linden. "Whether intentional, accidental, or out of ignorance, it needs to be addressed by the FAA."

The three of us talked for another hour and we decided that we would start a database and begin tracking laser illuminations against any commercial, military, private, or law enforcement aircraft.

Now all I had to do was get the word out. I drove on the I-10 West heading back to the CASFO.

· · ·

Six months later, I was nervous as I stood before nine FAA Aviation Security regional managers about to give a security briefing about laser threats. This was my first briefing for any manager. Don Harding, my immediate manager, and the Western-Pacific Region division manager asked me to talk about this at their annual meeting which was being held in San Diego, California.

It will be okay, Maggie, you got this.

My power point presentation was met with skepticism and humor. I don't think one person in the room believed that a tiny beam of light from a laser pointer directed at the cockpit area of a helicopter or aircraft could cause the pilot any harm.

Not remotely what I expected and not what the division manager for the Western-Pacific Region expected either.

"Thanks, Maggie," Don said. "I know this information is new to everyone here. We, in Western-Pacific, plan to keep tracking laser incidents and will update everyone from now on. We think this is an emerging threat and needs to be tracked."

I left the conference room with mixed feelings. *Well, at least no one patted me on the head or totally debunked what I was saying. But I had to admit, my briefing seemed to fall on deaf ears.*

Partly out of frustration and anger, I said to no one in particular, "Enough of this. I'm taking leave for the rest of the day." I decided to go see my sister who lived about thirty minutes from where my meeting was.

"Hey sis, got time for a walk?"

"Sure do, can't wait to see you. What's up, girl?"

"I need to vent. I just had the worst reaction to any security briefing I have ever done. It's a topic I've become an expert on, and the audience, my peers, looked at me like I was an idiot. I need my sister. Got time for a walk?"

"Absolutely. I'll meet you at Mission Bay in an hour."

. . .

The next day, driving home, thinking about my briefing, I wondered if there was anything I could have done differently. I stressed the danger, the potential harm to pilots--especially commercial pilots who had passengers to protect too. It was all there, a solid timeline, facts, and documented incidents, not only from Ontario Airport, but other airports throughout California, Nevada, Arizona, and others. It was a growing threat, not a diminishing one. And my dismissal as a town crier really pissed me off!

Guess I needed to talk to other people besides my own organization.

. . .

And for the next eighteen months that's exactly what I did. At every opportunity I gave briefings, presentations, and continued to collect data. At every opportunity I worked with law enforcement agencies and government officials to help them understand the growing threat of lasers.

Finally, after informally tracking laser incidents for years, the Federal Aviation Administration established a mechanism to record laser incidents through its operation center in Washington, D.C. Now when a pilot reports a lasing incident to the center, they in turn contact the FBI and local law enforcement agencies.

However, the regulatory efforts had stalled. A specific federal laser strike statute was still pending but there didn't seem to be any urgency to get it out for public comment and then published.

"Come on, you guys, what's the hold up? I've given you the draft regulation for 39A, Aiming a laser pointer at an aircraft. I know what I'm doing; I used to work in policy and planning."

"Then you know everything takes time, Maggie," Charlotte Biggs, branch manager from our D.C. Operations Division said.

"Well, how about publishing the advisory circular I wrote? We can do that internally. I'll come to D.C. on a detail, Charlotte, and co-ordinate it with Flight Standards and Air Traffic. At least we'll be able to advise the aviation community on the threat and how to mitigate it."

"I'll kick that idea around, Maggie, and get back to you ASAP."

CHAPTER **8**

Becoming Number Two

"I'm so glad everyone waits until Friday for me to sign off on cases," I complained to Agent Stanton over coffee.

"It comes with the job, Maggie. Remember how we used to do the same thing to Supervisor Drake," Stanton said with a chuckle.

"I sure do. Man-oh-man he used to get so mad when he'd come in Friday morning, his in-box spilling over, filled with cases that we put there Thursday after he left work for the day."

"I know you don't get mad," Stanton said, "but I bet your agents, and your two supervisors have fun messing with you too. Welcome to management."

"Where is Drake now?"

"After you moved to D.C. he left the FAA and went to work for the IRS. I understand he's based somewhere near Laguna Niguel. I heard through the grapevine that he took a lateral transfer, but is a lot happier with the work hours, and he's about fifteen minutes from his house. It's a gravy commute for him. And from what I understand he's really good at his job."

"Good for him. I'm glad he's happy."

"I'm off to a meeting so I'll catch-up with you later."

"See you. Thanks for stopping by and letting me rant."

"Anytime, Maggie, anytime."

After reviewing the twenty-five cases that were neatly stacked beside the in-box on the credenza beside my desk, I signed off on the 2150 and carried them to the assistant's desk who would make copies of the 2150, Section A and B and then forward them to the regional office. There they would review them again and, if they were satisfied the case was properly written, i.e. the correct FARs were cited, and the case would then be forwarded to legal. After a case went to legal we seldom heard any more about it. That was a bone of contention for our agents since many of them wondered if the inspections and investigations they were doing were actually being processed by legal.

Occasionally we received a list of cases that were administratively closed due to exceeding the two-year time period for processing. When that happened the agents in the office would grumble for days. Can't say I blamed them, I didn't like it either. It felt like a loophole that the regulated parties hoped would happen so they wouldn't have to pay any type of civil penalty, and/or, the case wouldn't appear in their enforcement record in the automated system legal kept.

The agents had strict guidelines they were required to follow if they discovered a potential violation and opened an investigation against an airport operator, airline, or individual. The guidelines were so strict that if the timelines were not met agents could be disciplined. So when cases came back because they went stale while waiting for legal to process them, our agents went ballistic.

Their outrage was another reason why I, too, grumbled under my breath every time I saw a stack of cases on my desk. I didn't want to be a part of the cog that slowed the process down. The sooner I reviewed and signed off on them, the sooner they got through the regional office and onto an attorney's desk.

I spent most of the day in my office reviewing cases, approving time cards, and attending two staff meetings. Friday was usually the day I tried to clear any pending items off my desk and my appointment calendar, which at least gave me a chance at beginning the new work week with a clean slate.

At 3:30 P.M. I called home to check on the kids. No one answered, which wasn't unusual. Monica was fourteen now and Mike twelve. They were very self-sufficient and probably didn't mind one bit that I worked long hours. I didn't worry too much. I trusted them both beyond words. I was blessed to have two wonderful kids.

I'd be leaving in thirty-minutes. I'd see them soon enough.

Picking up my briefcase, grabbing my jacket off the back of my chair, I headed for the door. Then my desk telephone rang. Putting down my belongings, I walked over and picked up the line with the blinking light.

"Hello, this is Maggie Stewart."

"Hi Maggie. Tom here. I have some good news for you," he said.

"Great, I can always use good news at quitting time," I replied.

Tom had this amazing habit of calling every Friday just as I was about to walk out of the office. Usually he wanted to pontificate about something; a case, an idea, asking how my week went, anything. I admired his dedication, but lingering in the back of my mind I always felt like he was checking up on the office. *God love Tom.* Today, I especially wanted to go home because I had a date!

At a joint terrorism meeting last week the key speaker, Jim Peppers, California emergency management crisis coordinator and I met. We hit it off right away and we'd been on the phone ever since. Jim lived in San Luis Obispo. As our relationship grew with excitement and anticipation, we soon realized the three hour commute kept us apart. We decided to meet halfway, in Santa Barbara at noon on Saturday. I was more than anxious to get out the door for the weekend. My boss, on the other hand, wanted to chat.

"I've selected you to be my deputy. The selecting panel was unanimous and D.C. signed off on your selection this morning," Tom said cheerfully.

"That's great news. Thanks so much, Tom. I'm looking forward to the opportunity."

"Stop by the regional office Monday to pick up your personnel action and let's discuss your new duties. Have a nice weekend."

"I will and thanks again. I really appreciate this opportunity."

. . .

Bubbling with excitement over the job promotion and with meeting Jim, I walked into an empty house. I could feel my excitement dissipate and turn into curiosity. *Where they heck was everyone?* Even our dog wasn't in the backyard.

The good news would have to wait. A few minutes later I dropped a note on the breakfast bar letting my kids know that I was out for a short run. I figured I could get four or five miles in before it was time to start cooking dinner.

"Hi guys. Hi Felipe," I said when I saw my kids sitting on the sofa eating chips and watching TV. "Ready for dinner?" I hollered from the hallway as I slipped off my running shoes and put on my flip-flops.

"We're starving," Mike replied.

"Well, you won't be if you eat all those chips. Turn off the TV and come help me get dinner ready and on the table. We're having spaghetti, garlic bread, and salad tonight."

"Cool, can Felipe stay too?"

"Call, ask your Mom, Felipe, if she says so it's okay."

During dinner I spent more time watching three hungry kids shovel food into their mouths than talking. The boys ate three plates of spaghetti and Monica two. Even the dog managed to get a few morsels of food, both intentionally and accidentally dropped on the tile kitchen floor. Leaning back in my chair, smiling, I was a very content mom.

"Hey, I've got a date tomorrow in Santa Barbara. Any chance you guys can hang out with friends tomorrow?"

"Who, Mom?" Mike asked.

"His name is Jim. We met at one of the anti-terrorism meetings I went to a couple of weeks ago. We've been talking on the phone ever since. We've set up a date tomorrow. Are you cool with that?"

"That's cool, Mom," Monica said. Mike only nodded his head but he wasn't scowling.

. . .

Monday became a blur of activity as soon as I walked in the door. My mind was still with Jim in Santa Barbara. It was a very romantic and picture perfect weekend. We went to Mass, walked along the harbor looking at boats, ate Mexican food, and drank a few bottles of wine. We had so much in common. Jim proposed and I accepted! Talk about a whirlwind romance. I was one hundred percent in love and I ready to spend the rest of my life with this intelligent and interesting man.

On the drive back to Redondo Beach my head was full of wedding plans, blending families, and driving the 101 highway until we could figure out a plan to manage our careers too.

At the office I began to understand the complexity and magnitude of the position I had just accepted. When you were a field office manager you only had one office to worry about. But when you became number two, the deputy division manager for the Western-Pacific you had to begin worrying about five field offices and approximately 150 agents and support staff.

"Here's your office, Maggie," Don Harding said to me after my meeting with Tom, Don, and Bob.

Don Harding was the director of operations. Craig Dillon was the director of internal investigations. These were two of the four direct report employees that now reported directly to me. The other two were the division secretary and the internet technician. Piece of cake you think, but when the region consists of 150 agents, support staff, and five field offices, the oversight is a tremendous responsibility.

FAA Security had grown exponentially in the past few years, though sadly by terrorist events and airline crashes, which created aviation security program expansions.

We had access control Special Emphasis Audits (SEAs), access investigations, pre-screening checkpoint tests, facility inspections in addition to our normal operational duties. Some of my ongoing responsibilities entailed making sure that the CASFO managers were getting the work assigned, completed, and any associated reports submitted on time. In addition, I began handling most of the personnel activities for the region.

As the work responsibilities increased, staffing levels decreased. Alan Manner transferred from the LAX CASFO to the regional office. Nadine Levor went to an instructor development course in Oklahoma City. Yolanda Freidman went to LDP1 training in Florida to become a supervisor. We had an airport workshop in San Diego, a DG HAZMAT Strike Team in Los Angeles for two weeks.

Aviation Security (AVSEC) Table Top Exercises were scheduled for six of our airports in one month. The airports, airlines, and FAA all participated in these exercises in preparation for a variety of accidents, security breaches, or terrorist attacks.

Walking into my new office, a converted closet actually, I could feel the responsibility surround me in this tiny windowless room; similar to being enclosed in a Sensitive Compartmented Information Facility, SCIF. My office didn't have any classified information as SCIFs do. The windowless design was identical, except I didn't have to show my identification every time I walked through the door.

Sitting down in the large chair behind my desk, when I placed my hands, fingers spread on top of my desk, I could feel and hear the vibration of the elevator moving between floors.

"It's not only a remodeled closet, you're right behind the main elevator shaft," Don informed me with a hardy chuckle.

"Don't you love government office space," I said. "This place is going to need some pictures."

CHAPTER 9

Soups On

"Boss, Boss, come quick, there's a fight in the conference room," Craig Dillon shouted.

"Really," I said, a tone carrying a note of slight disbelief.

"Yes ma'am, there is."

Immediately rising from my chair, I briskly walked toward the conference room, with Craig on my heels directly behind me. I could almost feel him breathing down my neck as we moved quickly down the narrow passageway between the agents' cubicles and the managers' office doors.

In my mind I wondered why Craig was asking me to break up a potential fight; he was a former body builder, naval investigator, and rode Harleys. He was the spitting image of tough. And here he was behind a woman half his size, looking like a nervous Nellie.

This couldn't be for real.

Staring into the conference room I almost laughed. Sitting at the long conference table, were two employees, not speaking, but clearly words had flown earlier – along with other things.

"Okay, what's going on here?"

Al and Joe both looked up at me and not a word was spoken.

"Well….," I said with my hands on my hips. I felt like a kindergarten teacher trying to extract from her fighting children what had happened.

"We got into an argument," Al said.

"I can see that. Are you two enjoying your lunch?"

Dripping, Al wiped the green oozing pea soup off his forehead with the back of his hand. Then he wiped his brow and right cheek and angrily glanced over at Joe.

"Actually, it was his lunch and he dumped it on my head," he said, pointing his index finger at Joe.

Looking at Joe I said, "So what happened?"

Joe began, "We were talking about the upcoming elections and we got into an argument."

"It's your fault, Joe," Al blurted out.

"No, it's your fault. You're the one who's always shoving your opinion down everyone's throat."

"And in this case on someone's face," Joe retorted.

"Okay, okay enough!" I said. "Here's what you two are going to do. Clean this mess up, clean yourselves up, and go home for the rest of the day. I'm putting you both on administrative leave. It's Friday so take the weekend to calm down and we'll talk again on Monday."

Nodding their heads was the only indication I saw that they had heard me.

"Craig will oversee the clean-up in here. Understood?"

"Yes," Al said.

"Okay, get this place cleaned up and I'll see the two of you in my office at 0800 hours on Monday."

Turning around, I brushed past Craig and headed back toward my office.

. . .

"Hi Stanton." I sat down at the table for lunch at the local Mexican restaurant on Aviation Boulevard. The food here was good, cheap, and the location was exactly halfway between the regional office and the airport, which made it easy for both Lee and me. "You aren't going to believe how my day's been so far."

"What happened?"

After ordering plates of tacos, rice, and beans and munching on fresh chips, with the hottest salsa we could find, I recounted the 'pea soup' story.

Twenty-minutes later, pushing back our nearly empty plates, I knew I had eaten too much.

"Did it again," I said, patting my well-fed stomach.

While reaching for his wallet, Agent Stanton nodded in agreement. We sat in silence while the waiter brought over the bill. I knew there wasn't much that could surprise Agent Stanton, but the pea soup incident had him speechless.

"What are you going to do about it?"

"Give them the weekend to sweat a little, you know; what is the deputy going to do to them, sleepless night stuff. Don's out on leave, so once he hears what they have to say, I'll let him decide. They're his employees. I got involved because he was gone."

"Well, good luck. Monday I'm meeting with the FBI about our upcoming joint airport vulnerability assessment at LAX. I think we're going to need to adjust the assessment methodology like you did for Honolulu back in February."

"What time is that meeting again, Lee? Want me to tag along if I'm free?"

"Sure, it's at eleven A.M. You'll probably be done with your two knuckleheads by then. The FBI meeting is at my office."

. . .

"Good morning, Lord," I mumbled after hitting the snooze alarm for the third time. Even the Sandhill Crane alarm sounded tired on this foggy Monday morning.

Coffee made, note on the breakfast bar for the kids to take out the trash cans, Sandee patted on the head, I walked in the garage and got into my Jeep. Backing out I started my very short commute to the office.

I lived less than two miles from work and every time I got in my car I felt a pang of guilt, knowing that I should be walking instead of dumping more fumes into this already delicate atmosphere of Mother Earth. Over the years I'd tried a few alternative means to get to work like riding a bike, walking, even using a scooter for about six months. I'd been chased by dogs, drenched by sprinklers, and scared by close calls with cars at the few intersections between home and office. After each incident I'd beat a hasty retreat to my beloved Jeep and drive the short commute, grateful I was still alive. In my opinion, traffic wasn't much different in Redondo Beach than anywhere else in California.

Parking in the last row at the office I smugly smiled knowing I'd walk further than anyone else from the parking lot to my desk.

"Good morning," I said to the security guard as I showed him the identification badge that hung around my neck. After gaining access into the building, I walked down the long hallway toward the lobby. The hallway walls were dotted with various photos of aviation milestones. Color, black and white, and several posters, hung in chronological order, displaying the advancement and achievements of man's desire to fly or explore space.

I'd loved airplanes for as long as I can remember. To still be involved in the aviation community was a great source of honor for me. And walking past these pictures every day gave me a sense of pride and joy. I still felt like a little kid every time I watched an airplane fly overhead or lift-off from a runway.

Before reaching the rectangle-shaped lobby, I pushed the door leading into the enormous stairwell for my climb from the ground level to the sixth floor.

I don't know what it was about the regional office stairs, but by the time I reached the top, I was always out of breath, feeling as if the sour air inside the stuffy stairwell would stay inside my lungs all day.

Maybe I should have taken the elevator because I always exited the west-facing stairwell by the regional operations center. *Nah, I'd be okay – I'd just keep distance-running via stairs.*

And every morning I stopped in at the operations center to pick up the mail: including classified and sensitive mail, if there was any.

"Good morning, Diana. How are you? Is there any mail for us?"

"I'm good. Thanks for asking. Nope, there's no mail today, Maggie."

I spent the next couple of hours responding to emails, reviewing personnel actions, and getting ready for the week ahead. I heard a faint tap at my door. When I looked up, Al and Joe were waiting to be invited into my office. I mentally noted the business suits.

Good first impression, gentlemen. At least they understood they were in hot water.

"Come on in and take a seat."

Here we go. This would be an interesting conversation.

"Don Harding will be here shortly," I said.

On cue, Don came into the office. Al and Joe reported to Don. Don looked the unhappiest of the three. Unhappy, because while he was on leave two of his agents had acted so foolishly. Getting the boss's boss involved was never a good thing.

"Okay, you two, for the benefit of your boss, explain yourselves."

Don glared at the two federal agents and listened.

Twenty minutes later the talking stopped. The two agents had told their story to their boss who had grown more and more agitated by the minute.

"That's it?" Don asked.

"Pretty much," Joe said.

"Okay, get back to work, you two. I'll have a decision by the end of the week."

As the two agents got up to leave, I said, "Close the door on the way out."

After the door creaked closed Don looked at me and said, "Well, what do you think?"

"I think they're a couple of knuckleheads and they deserve whatever action you take. Welcome back, Don."

After a short pause, I said, "Speaking of personnel, I need to take care of something."

. . .

I called Cecil in personnel and left a message. "Cecil, are you the right person in personnel to contact for a name change. I got married on Saturday, March 21st."

Leaning back in my chair I thought back to my wedding day. Jim and I got married after dating for only three months. It was a whirl-wind romance filled with long drives between San Luis Obispo and Redondo Beach to see one another. We hadn't resolved our long-distance relationship yet. But we had faith that one day we'd find a solution. Meanwhile our phone bills were outrageous. Our kids thought we were insane. And Jim and I were giddy with happiness.

The church, Wayfarers Chapel in Palos Verdes, was spectacular. Ocean views, magnificent windows—filled the chapel with sunshine and blue skies. It was a beautiful wedding and we were extremely happy and lucky to have found one another.

"Well, Well, Well!" Cecil wrote back a few hours later, "Congratulations! Have your administrative person, Linda or Garnetta, prepare and forward a name change personnel action to me. Also, forward a copy of your marriage license and I'll take care of it. Then for your Thrift Saving Plan and Health Benefit changes contact, Malinda Marquez at extension x7855. You'll be set."

CHAPTER **10**

October Skies

"Are you guys too old to trick or treat?"

"No, Mom. You're never too old to get free candy," my almost-teenage son hollered back from the living room.

"And I just want to go to a party, Mom. I'm not trick or treating, but I want to wear a costume."

"Okay, we've still got a couple weeks before Halloween, so let me know what you two decide to be and I'll see if I can afford it."

"The scarier the better for me," said my beyond-teenage-years daughter.

"I don't know yet, Mom. Maybe Pokémon like a little kid," Michael said with a laugh.

"Sounds good – love you – got to go or I'll be late for work."

Driving the very short commute to the office, again I felt guilty. I knew I should be walking or riding my bike to work, especially in October when the weather is perfect. No rain, no fog, no blistering hot summer days; just the cool sea air washing over the city, a gentle reminder from Mother Nature that California was one of the best places on earth to live.

I loved it here. However, I'd had my ups and downs in California. The downside was that the cost of living was outrageous. The traffic was a nightmare. The upside was the sunshine, beaches, and casual lifestyle. Somehow, someway I always migrated back to Southern California.

I'd had my ups and downs in relationships too. I felt an enormous pang of guilt about Jim. Within a few months of getting married, we hardly saw one another. Our time together drifted like the sands on a windy beach, as we figured out that I couldn't move to San Luis Obispo, 200 miles north on Hwy 101. Jim couldn't move south to Redondo Beach. We were a married couple, living apart. My kids didn't mind but I sure did. Working beyond full-time while trying to finish raising my kids was about all I could handle – my marriage came in third – and my husband was not a happy man. I wasn't happy either.

My work, my world, my life was rooted in Southern California. I'd move from time-to-time but I always came back. Native Californians, our family lived in Hollywood until divorce forced us from the home we grew up in. After a bitter, sad, and lengthy court battle, our Dad got custody of three very unruly children.

My parents were ferocious drinkers. I think they probably drank from the moment they realized that booze gave them the buzz they needed to get through each day. At least, I think that's what they thought at the time. My Mom would drink anything she could get her hands on, cheap wine, spirits, even mouthwash. My Dad, on the other hand, stuck to Scotch, except at dinner when he had a tall water glass of wine. Dad won custody only because he was less of a drunk than Mom was. And he was able to convince the court that he would take better care of us. As mean spirited, bitter, and caustic as Dad was most of the time, it was true. True that he could, would, and did do a better job of taking care of us – but only by the grace of God – because he called in reinforcements to help.

After several moves, we finally settled in Seal Beach, California and our Grandmother Irene came to live with us. She came at my dad's request.

Grandma Irene, I am sure, who was happily retired, did not care to relocate to California. She was living in a small upstairs apartment, very close to the California state capitol in Sacramento, where she no doubt came and went as she wanted, had a multitude of friends, and loved her walks in the bustling city every day.

But Grandma Irene did move. And she was exactly what our dysfunctional family needed. *Sadly, when it came to relationships, I was rather dysfunctional.*

Turning into the regional office parking lot, I slapped my hand on my steering wheel. *Wow, how on earth did I get on this topic? October gloom. Gosh girl, get a grip. October gloom was seeping into my bones. But it would be okay. Somehow it would be okay.*

By the time I climbed the stairs to the sixth floor I was huffing and puffing, completing forgetting about my recent decision to divorce Jim...and my gloomy childhood memories. It was time to focus on the morning staff meeting which Tom held every morning at 8:30 A.M. *At least I was an expert at work.* That comforted me while I said good morning to the staff.

. . .

"Did you vet this personnel action with legal, Don," Tom asked, glancing at the proposed personnel actions that were sitting on his desk awaiting his signature.

"Yes, it's within the scope of the personnel regulations, Tom."

"Good, but I'd like it redrafted for Maggie's signature, please, since she handles all of the personnel actions now."

"Yes sir."

Tom turned back to me, "Have you read the drafts?"

"Yes, I concur. They could have been suspended for up to thirty days. Since this is the first offense I think a five day suspension is more in line than a reprimand. We need to send a message that fighting of any kind, even if its pea soup dumping, is not a behavior becoming of special agents."

"Agreed," Don said, as Tom nodded his head.

"Linda, what's the status on the budget-continuing resolution?

"It's bleak, Tom. The CR is based on last year's budget minus ten percent."

"Let's meet after this meeting, Linda, to discuss in more detail."

Turning to Dan Martinez, Tom said, "Dan, anything to report this morning?"

"Yes. The government accounting office (GAO) is coming back to look at physical security again. They want to see if we're following through with our survey and inspections commitment. And Dave, the team leader, said they'd probably be looking at the quality of our work product, i.e., reports, surveys, and assessments."

"Okay. Keep Harding and Nuggett in the loop on this."

Tap, tap, tap – the door opened – Karen stuck her head in and said, "Sorry to interrupt, but JJ called and said you should switch on CNN, Tom. There's an unfolding incident on TV."

Thanking Karen, Tom reached behind his desk, grabbed the remote, and turned on the television.

CNN was reporting that a Learjet carrying golfer Payne Stewart had gone off their intended flight path and air traffic was not able to contact the pilots flying the aircraft.

"I wonder what's going on inside that bird," Craig Dillon said, staring at the TV.

"Don't know, Craig, but I bet it's not good," I replied.

Continuing to watch the TV, Tom called the operations center, "JJ, Tom here. Anything else you can tell us about this flight?"

"No, Tom. I'm monitoring Washington, D.C., Central Operations Watch, and Air Traffic all in mute mode, so if I hear anything I'll make sure you know first, sir."

"Thanks, JJ. Appreciate it."

CNN was now reporting that an Air Force F-16 from the 40th Flight Test Squadron at Eglin AFB in western Florida had been dispatched to intercept the aircraft. The pilot of the F-16 had made two radio calls to N47BA but did not get a response. The pilot reported that he made a visual inspection of the aircraft and both engines were running, and the plane's red, rotating anti-collision beacon was on.

"Having the anti-collision beacon on is a standard operating procedure for a Lear," Tom said.

A half hour later, after watching the Lear pilot flying through hundreds of miles of airspace that he wasn't supposed to be in, the F-16 pilot reported that after multiple angles and attempts he could not clearly see into the cockpit or the cabin since the windshield was opaque, or perhaps thinly covered with condensation or ice.

We ended our staff meeting and I walked down to the conference room where the majority of our agents had gathered to watch CNN.

"Maggie," Rich said, "I don't know if you've been watching this, but the news is now reporting that there's some speculation that the military jet is prepared to shoot down the Lear if it threatens to crash in a heavily populated area."

"Any response back from the pilots yet?"

"No, none," Rich said.

Everyone in the conference room was riveted to the television. It was as if time had stopped. You knew a tragedy was unfolding and you were completely mystified as to why. Even more frustrating was knowing you couldn't do a darn thing about it.

CNN began reporting that the Lear began a right turn and descent. The aircraft looked like it was out of control, descending in a spiral toward the earth.

Sadly, almost four hours into Stewart Payne's flight, impact occurred on a relatively flat piece of land just outside of Mina, South Dakota killing everyone onboard.

Not a word was uttered. Sitting in absolute silence, we were numb and stunned.

. . .

Monday turned into Tuesday, and Tuesday into Wednesday. When Friday arrived I could tell the entire office was more than ready to escape these federal walls that held them five days a week.

"Go, get out of here everyone," I shouted out from my office door. "I'm granting the 59 minute rule, so scram."

Fifty-nine minutes of administrative leave could be granted to any employee when a manager deemed it appropriate. The FAA usually implemented this policy before a holiday, bad weather, or perhaps to get a jump on a specific bad traffic situation. It's not used very often, so when the word got around, everyone scrambled for the door, happily escaping into the parking lot.

"Go, Karen, you need to go home too. I'll stay and answer phones."

"Thanks, Maggie. I could use the time. I need to grocery shop. My son has a football game tonight."

"Hope they win."

"I do too. Thanks again. See you Monday."

CHAPTER 11

Trick or Treat

"Where is everybody? Anybody up yet," I shouted as I walked in the front door. My shirt was sticky, sweaty, and felt awful, but my heart, brain, and feet were marvelous. There was nothing like a 10-mile run to start off a Sunday morning.

I went to 5:00 P.M. Mass Saturday night so I could train early Sunday morning. I was hooked on distance running and I had signed up for another marathon. This one was in San Francisco. And fortunately, my alarm clock worked and obviously I was able to get out the door, run, and return before my two lovely children were even awake.

After showering and eating a banana, I stood watching the dog sleeping. I heard stirrings beginning upstairs. My son came downstairs looking sleepy.

"What's for breakfast, Mom?"

"Well good morning, to you too, kiddo. How about some pancakes?"

The scent of bacon lured Monica downstairs and soon we were all happily eating a rare meal together.

"So what did you guys decide to wear tomorrow for Halloween?"

"I'm going as a witch," Monica said.

Glancing over at Mike I said, "Don't even think about saying what I know you're thinking, son."

Mike laughed, "Okay. And I'm going as a hobo."

"Really? Why?" I asked.

"So I can carry a pillow-case and get a lot of candy, Mom!"

"Dork brother," Monica chimed in.

"Hey, I didn't call you a real-live-witch, did I? So leave me alone – witch!"

"Okay, okay you two – chill out. Help me do the dishes."

. . .

That didn't sound like my alarm clock. The telephone on my night stand continued its shrill ringing.

"Hello," I croaked, looking at my wrist watch and seeing that it was 4:00 A.M.

"Maggie, its Diana from the operations center. I'm patching you in with Tom Thomas and the D.C. Operations Center. There's been a crash in New York."

"Okay, standing by," I said getting out of bed, grabbing my bath-robe, and heading downstairs to grab a pen and paper. Switching on the kitchen light I turned on the coffee pot, let the sleepy dog out, and sat down at the kitchen table, listening while telephone lines clicked as various communication lines were established around the country.

Once roll call was taken by Washington we were briefed that Egypt Air 998 had departed Los Angeles, California at 11:00 P.M. enroute to New York. The same aircraft, now identified as flight Egypt Air 990, had departed John F. Kennedy (JFK) Airport at 1:19 A.M. and went off radar at 2:00 A.M.

Before the flight disappeared, an SOS was sent approximately 45 miles off of Nantucket. No word yet on the crew or passengers.

"Tom, I want your region to set up a command post there in LA since the flight originated from there," Lee Levi directed.

"Roger that," Tom replied to the director of operations for our organization.

Once D.C. clicked off the line I advised Tom that I was on my way to the office. Don Harding and Mac McMullen told Tom they on their way to the office too.

"Okay everyone, I'll see you when I get there, which will be in about an hour."

After quickly getting ready for work, I wrote a note for the kids, let the dog back in, grabbed my coffee, and headed for the office.

. . .

An eerie silence enveloped me as I stepped out of the elevator on the 5th floor of the regional office building. The dimly lit hallway was spooky. I could see my shadow looming against the battleship gray door. Putting my master key into the locked security door, I felt the handle turn, as my thoughts turned toward the gloomy day ahead.

I dropped my briefcase in the office chair, walked over to the small kitchen area and began making a pot of coffee. *At least I could make the coffee my way*. I dropped a copious amount of coffee grounds into the filter, turned on the giant machine, and headed back to my desk.

Gradually the staff: Don, Mac, Larry, Al, Karen T., and Tom came in.

After filling his coffee-stained mug Tom headed to the conference room to begin our emergency meeting.

Within an hour we recapped what we knew about Egypt Air 990, established a command post at the regional office that would be managed by Don Harding, and would establish the forward command post at the airport.

"Maggie, Luz Pase is in Palm Coast, Florida so I need you to run the forward command post," Tom said. "I just spoke with Agent Stanton and he's agreed that we can use his office. Organize your team and notify Don after you do."

"I'll take Rich, Lori, Alex, Matt, Karen T., and Roy," I said immediately.

"Okay, let's get to work."

. . .

"Thanks for letting us use your office, Stanton."

"No problem, Maggie. D.C. told us that Egypt Air 990 went down about sixty miles offshore from Massachusetts after departing from JFK. There appear to be no survivors. D.C. wants a forward command post here in L.A. because the flight originated from LAX. Our FAA Eastern Region is establishing one too."

"I understand that air traffic lost contact shortly after the plane took off and left New York airspace. The Mode C transponder showed plane lost altitude rapidly which probably means that some type of failure occurred on the plane. Now we need to figure out what and why."

"Why. Always the million dollar question," Agent Gordon said.

"We need to look at ground handling, ticket counter, baggage, and cargo. Probably the security checkpoint at the Tom Bradley International Terminal (TBIT) too," I said. "So, I want you Alex and Matt at the checkpoint, Lori at ticket counter, Roy at cargo and, Rich you need to look at baggage and talk to the station manager."

"Let's go talk to the Egypt air station manager first, Rich," Lee suggested.

"Good idea. And I want checkpoint tests run immediately too."

"Agreed, it's best to conduct our testing and interviews before too much time passes. We can decide who to interview after we talk to the station manager. He'll be able to give us the names of who was on duty."

"Let's all meet back here at thirteen hundred hours to debrief and see what we're missing. Any questions?" I asked.

Noting none, Stanton said, "Okay, let's go. We've got a few people to have a chat with."

A few hours later Rich Gordon faxed the passenger manifest from the Egypt air station manager to Washington.

The team decided to test all the equipment in the Tom Bradley Terminal (TBIT), at the south and north checkpoints. The testing resulted in two failures. Both were failures to recognize an encapsulated gun at the ankle level.

Alex and Matt conducted testing on the five metal detectors; three primary, two secondary, along with three x-ray machines at both checkpoints.

"After all the testing was complete, we had two failures," Alex reported.

"Where?" Stanton demanded.

"At the north checkpoint, two at the ankle level. I got the roster of the screeners too."

"Good work."

"The equipment was certified last April," Matt added. "I got the explosive trace detection (ETD) records."

"Okay, equipment certification is fine. Let me know if you find any discrepancies with the paperwork."

"How many flights a week does Egypt Air have out of LAX Stanton?" I asked.

"Two."

"Any selectees on 990?" I asked.

"No, none," Rich replied. "None of the passengers had been selected for secondary screening, Maggie."

"Okay. What else do we need to look at?"

After recapping the information and testing results we decided that we needed to interview not only the station manager, but the supervisors on duty, ground crew, ticket counter, and cleaning personnel.

. . .

"Morning, Maggie," Lee said as I walked into his office early Saturday morning.

"Good morning. Don't you ever go home, Agent Lee Stanton?" I chuckled.

Sipping his coffee, Lee only smiled.

"I stopped at the RO before coming here and the FBI is sending a team here later this morning. I talked to Sam Stanton, FBI Office in L.A. and Agent Dave Baker is the lead."

"Well, it's about time they showed up. I've been waiting."

"Me too."

When the rest of our team gathered, Roy and Tony reported that the pallet cargo locations, baggage loading, and bulk loads had been identified. The HAZMAT records were being reviewed by Angela.

"I've collected the passenger and crew bag tag information," Lori advised. "And Rich is starting the bag match process."

At 10:00 A.M., the team of FBI agents arrived. After introductions were made, a very preliminary briefing of what our FAA security agents had discovered during investigating was discussed. The jam-packed room was warming up quickly and it was obvious that we were going to need more space.

"I'll find another office, Maggie," Lee said as he picked up the phone and began punching in numbers.

Thirty minutes later we moved to a large conference room located on the third floor of the Tom Bradley International Terminal. The LAX Airport had an executive conference room there and we could use it for as long as we needed.

"Head home, guys. Try and get some sleep," I said. "See you all tomorrow at 2 P.M. Thanks for all the hard work."

Teams had been formed, each working twelve-hour shifts, but Stanton and I continued to work close to eighteen hours a day. We had enough time away from the command center to eat, change our clothes, hug our families and come back to work. Our bodies ran on adrenaline, our minds on wit, cooperation, and grit.

Several days later, after a full day, Stanton and I stayed a few more hours and then headed home ourselves. I needed to see my children, if only while they were sleeping.

Thankfully they were old enough now to spent time on their own. Latch key kids wasn't a new phrase--sadly it was true, and I hated it. I missed talking to them. I missed seeing their smiles and hearing them laugh. But at least I knew they were okay. I slipped into my soft tub hot spa, glass of wine in hand, in an attempt to slow down from an incredibly exhausting week.

The following day was more of the same but with an added twist. The FBI wanted to interview everyone, not just the airline employees that had contact with Egypt Air 990. After lengthy discussion, Stanton and I decided it would be of mutual benefit if we teamed our agents up with the FBI agents.

"I agree, that's a solid plan," Agent Baker said. "We defer to your aviation expertise. Conducting interviews together will assure us that we get the information we need."

"Let's pair your agents with the existing security teams we have; ticket counter, screening, ramp, gate, baggage, CTX, cargo, aircraft. I'll notify the team leads that one of your agents will be joining."

"Great," Agent Baker said. "Much appreciated."

Lee glanced at Maggie. He said, I'm going over to Nancy Clark's office to brief her on our joint investigation and then to the monthly consortia meeting."

"Okay, Stanton. I'll hold the fort down here, and I'll call if anything significant happens."

At the morning briefing I asked, "Rich, how's the baggage match going?"

"Hudson General has helped me account for all of the baggage except for four bags," he said. "I understand those bags were checked in late and they had handwritten tags. We're still looking for where those bags were placed in the cargo hold. No records are kept for the flight crew bags and they don't have bag tags either. The crew handles their bags, so we're pretty much out of luck on determining how many bags they had. And don't forget company material (COMAT). That's another mystery since COMAT isn't on any manifest. It's usually aircraft spare parts carried onboard by the airline."

"What's the process again with the bags, Rich? I mean, how do they get from the passenger and onto the airplane?"

"After the passenger checks in, the passenger takes their bag upstairs to be x-rayed in front of the ticket counter. Once their bag is x-rayed and cleared Hudson General takes their bag back downstairs. The bags get held until the passengers begin boarding the aircraft. Once everyone is onboard and the passenger bag match is complete the flight is good to go."

I nodded and looked at Angela, asking how the interviews were going.

"The FBI teamed up in pairs with our agents. Lori, Shandra, Jose, Walt, Alex, Amy, Alan, Mark, Garrick, and Susan are conducting interviews. We should have an updated report at our four P.M. briefing today. "

"Okay. Good. Do you know how many interviews they've done so far?"

"Around forty, which is about half of what they anticipate doing. They are interviewing, or re-interviewing everyone again - ticket counter, gate, cargo, baggage room, ramp, checkpoint, CTS, even the aircraft and the catering folks. So I think they have a ways to go."

"What are the citizenship stats, Alan?"

"One hundred six U.S. citizens, sixty-two Egyptians, two Sudanese, and twenty-two Canadians," he replied.

I recapped what we had discussed and ended our meeting.

Bag match, crew bags, and COMAT were the three worries at this point. We needed to find those bags. I began writing up the morning situation report (SITREP) for the regional office.

.   .   .

"Found it, Maggie," Rich said excitedly into the telephone. "It's here behind the ticket counter."

"That's outstanding. I'll be right there."

"You are amazing and you're the hero of this investigation, Rich. How the heck did you find it?" I said, standing at the Egypt Air ticket counter.

"I was talking to one of the ticket agents and she began explaining that the check-in process for the first class passengers was different than for business or coach. She told me that the first class bags are loaded last and taken off first so those customers always get their bags first at their arriving destination. "

"Okay, but why is that significant?"

"Because when the bags are loaded last they are sometimes held here at the ticket counter. So I looked – and lo and behold – there was a bag sitting here that no one bothered to look at."

"You are a clever man. Thanks, Rich. D.C. is going to be extremely happy when they find out we've reconciled all of the baggage here," I said, shaking his hand.

. . .

Two days later, the FBI was gone. They disappeared as quietly as they appeared ten days before, in their business suits, shiny shoes, and sunglasses. Agent Stanton and I commented on their professional attire and our more casual approach in dress. Working closely with the FBI was a tremendous experience. Both agencies blended as a team--each agency supporting the other. Our aviation expertise, their incredible interview skills, brought the Egypt Air 990 investigation to a close.

Every piece of baggage had been accounted for, cargo loads, COMAT, even a tire that Delta Airline had taken off the Egypt Air flight at their request prior to departing Los Angeles.

Two weeks of relentless, around the clock investigative work had resulted in having most of our security team standing in the TBIT lobby watching an Egypt Air B-767 lift off and make a gentle turn eastward toward New York.

CHAPTER 12

Threats and Turmoil

"A Southwest B-737 got moved to the remote parking pad, Maggie," Agent Stanton said hurriedly into the phone. "We got a specific bomb threat so get some agents out here ASAP."

"Roger that."

I picked up the phone, dialed Luz Pase, LAX CASFO manager and quickly explained what was going on and that Agent Stanton was requesting agents at the airport ASAP."

"Okay, Maggie, I'll contact the duty agent and we'll get a couple of agents out there," Luz said.

"Thanks, keep me posted when you can and I'll keep D.C. off your back. I'll call the operations center and get the notification process going."

After I hung up, I called the operations center and advised them that we had a specific bomb threat against a Southwest Airlines flight out of LAX and that a team was responding to assist Agent Stanton.

"Roger that, Maggie," Diana said.

I looked at my watch, noted the time, and wrote in my notebook that I had received this information at 8:00 P.M. and who was responding to the incident.

At 9:00 P.M. K-9 dogs from the Los Angeles Police Department responded and searched every piece of luggage, and the aircraft. Nothing was found and the incident was cleared at 11:30 P.M.

I found out the following morning that an individual had called the Southwest Airlines reservation system, specifically named the flight number, destination, and said there was a bomb onboard the aircraft.

The FBI was able to trace the call from a telephone at the LAX Airport, Terminal One--a pay phone. An individual had shown up late for the flight, was denied boarding, and was very upset with the airline. He was being held for questioning by the airport police, and the FBI. Agent Stanton, Federal Security Manager (FSM), was there as well.

· · ·

"Barry Mawn, FBI lead investigator said the guy is probably going to serve some jail time after pulling a stunt like that last night," Stanton said during lunch.

"The cost to the airline, the airport, and the government is tremendous," I said, chewing on my deli sandwich. "People have no idea how easy it is to get caught too," I said between bites.

"How's coverage for New Year's, Maggie?"

"Luz has agents assigned to all the terminals at LAX. She's going to call you later today. She's got her other airports covered too. And I've got the region covered. I'm almost done with the Egypt Air 990 report for D.C. Want to look it over before I send it up?"

"Sure, I'll get you what I wrote for my bosses in D.C. too."

"I still can't figure out why D.C. wants our office to write a second report. We both covered the incident. We both watched the flights resume – you know what I'm saying – been there, done that, so why separate reporting?"

"Come on," said Stanton. You know the drill; two bosses, yours and mine. They both want the information directly from their employee. Even if significant activity reports (SITREP) are verbatim in both."

"I hear you, but it makes me crazy," I said.

· · ·

"Okay, Maggie, I know this is getting old," said Stanton, but I need a couple of your agents to head out to the remote pad again. This time we've got an America West flight diverted from Phoenix with a passenger trying to get into the cockpit."

"Okay, I'll get some agents rolling and advise the operations center."

"Airport police and the FBI are rolling too."

Several hours later Matt Pellet and Lori Hope returned to the CASFO and called me.

Picking up my home telephone, I recognized the operations center number, "Stewart here."

"Maggie, its Matt and Lori and we're on speaker."

Grabbing a pen and my note pad, I said, "Go ahead."

"America West flight 90 diverted to LAX from Phoenix when a Middle Eastern man tried to get into the cockpit by beating and pulling on the door. He was unsuccessful. Some of the passengers made sure of that.

The pilots made an emergency landing at LAX and were directed to the remote pad by air traffic control. The FBI and LAX PD met the flight. We were there with Agent Stanton too," Lori said.

"After the man was arrested America West reported that the passenger had paid in cash, one-way ticket, and didn't have any luggage."

"Okay, that's not good," I said.

"I know. The plane was completely emptied," Matt added. "Bomb squad responded and searched the entire aircraft and every passenger's luggage. The FBI interviewed all of the passengers."

"Nothing was found during the search. All the passengers were re-boarded, except the unruly passenger. He's being detained for further questioning by the FBI."

I nodded. "Okay, I'll call this in to D.C. Excellent work, you two. And cc me and Luz on the SITREP when it's done. BTW Luz will be back in the office next week. I'll be sure to advise Luz on the excellent job you two did tonight. Thanks again."

. . .

Luz Pase had been the LAX CASFO manager for about six months when Egypt Air went down. And she was attending a two-week management training course in Florida when all hell broke loose in L.A. That's why I ran the forward command post.

Quietly sitting in my office I had a moment to study her. I was the one that had selected her as my replacement at the CASFO when I was promoted to the deputy division manager. I liked Luz a lot. She was cool under pressure, knew the regulations, and wasn't afraid to apply them. She was well liked by her peers and she was always professional. She was born and raised in Puerto Rico. Her slight accent made her deep voice rich, smooth and interesting. Her voice almost sang when she spoke. She dressed impeccably and every hair, shade of makeup was perfect. *I should dress more like Luz,* I thought every time I saw her. *Polished, professional, and spectacular.*

I turned to her. "Let's review this report together. We've got to hit the send button on this today. Agent Stanton has his report in and D.C. is beginning to question why I haven't submitted mine yet."

Without saying a word, she nodded, slipped on her reading glasses and quietly began reading the report.

"I found a couple of grammatical errors, Maggie. Do you mind if I correct them?

"No, not at all. Here, I'll trade places with you."

Forty-five minutes later I hit the send button. I cc'd Agent Stanton and my boss, Tom Thomas.

"Better late than never," I said. "Thanks, Luz, you really helped me a ton today. I was behind the power curve—that's for sure—on this one."

"I'm glad to help and I know how busy you are too. Do you mind if I ask how the personnel issue in the Phoenix CASFO is going?"

"Frankly, it's a mess. I'm afraid I'm going to have to suspend some agents."

. . .

A week later I suspended three agents from the PHX CASFO for time and attendance fraud, abuse of overtime, misuse of government vehicles, gambling on duty, preferential treatment of certain employees, interfering with government contracts, soliciting gifts from contractors, using racial, gender, and sexual preference slurs.

I told Tom Thomas, Don Harding, Gene Langer, and Craig Dillon about the mess. "And it's not enough – time off – they should all be fired," I added.

"Now, now Maggie, legal reviewed all of the evidence," Tom said.

"I know that. I just don't like it. Gene and Bob worked for six months investigating these allegations. The Report of Investigation (ROI) is five inches thick. And we get three thirty day suspensions and a reassignment out of it. That's it?"

No one said a word.

"And now we get rewarded by having to go to sensitivity training. Yep, that will help a lot."

. . .

Several months later, walking in my front door I shouted. "Hey guys, I'm home. Did you miss me? What's for dinner," I said with a laugh as my son and daughter gawked at me. "I don't know about you but I'm having wine – wine while I whine."

We unanimously agreed on pizza, take-out pizza with piping hot bread sticks slathered in butter and parmesan cheese, salad, and a liter of diet Coke.

After I downed my first glass of Chardonnay, I poured a second and began to feel like I was slowing down a bit. These past few months I had been putting in ten- to twelve-hour days, five days a week and sometimes six or seven. I knew I was on the verge of burning out, but work was work – a four letter word – without a doubt at times. And I knew I hadn't been home very much and when I was home I wasn't paying attention to anyone half the time. Thank God I had perfect children!

The administrative hearing that took place after I suspended four agents for various acts of misconduct was over. The ruling was in favor of the FAA but at what expense? The cost to defend my actions was enormous in staffing hours and tax payer dollars.

So how'd your week go Maggie? I took a trip to Phoenix today. Why? Did I help the traveling public any today? Did I help the agency any today? Probably not!

I listened to an administrative law judge. I rearranged a table and some chairs for Judge Toole. I made a couple of telephone calls for Denise Knapp, our attorney.

Did I help my family today? Probably not! Pizza for dinner doesn't seem to be enough. I told them I loved them. I know they love me.

Did I help myself today? Probably not much! I learned a few procedural points about administrative hearings. I learned how to jay-walk in Phoenix and not get a ticket. I watched a lot, listened a lot, and talked very little. I didn't run, I didn't get a good night's sleep, I myself didn't help much.

I supported my boss, but look at everything I gave up today to make that happen.

I'd given a lot up in my personal relationships too. I felt terrible divorcing Jim. We'd been married eighteen months. In that time we barely saw one another. A weekend here or there was about it. I never imagined our lives would be so busy and so separate. We reviewed every possible option, but I couldn't move to San Luis Obispo, 200 miles north on Hwy 101, and he couldn't move south to Redondo Beach. Work! It defined us, it attracted us to one another, it fed and sustained us, yet it was the poison that kept us apart. We'd never lived together. He begged me not to file. I couldn't see the point of staying married. I longed for a relationship, not a symbol, a life, a lover, a dream come true. I filed.

Snapping out of my melancholy mood I hugged my kids and said, "Come on, let's walk to the corner and get some ice cream. We haven't done that in ages."

CHAPTER 13

Divert and Descend

"Hi Greg. Thanks for taking my call."

"Hi Maggie, I haven't talked to you in months. How are you? How are the kids?"

"Good, thanks, but growing up way too fast."

"How are you?"

"Busy."

"The reason I'm calling is that I have an agent here in the office that wants to be an air marshal. And I know there's a federal air marshal (FAM) school start in February. What's the process now that the program is voluntary?"

"Send me a letter of recommendation with his resume and I'll look it over. If we're interested we'll invite him to Atlantic City to interview."

"Okay."

"Tell him if he gets selected that his move from California to Atlantic City will be at his own expense. We don't have PCS money anymore. Once he completes training he'll be on the road 60% of the time. And he has return rights to the Western-Pacific Region in four years."

"Okay, I'll pass this information onto Craig and I'll get back to you. Thanks, Greg."

"Any time. Great talking with you."

After hanging up I wrote a few more notes about our conversation and sent Craig an email explaining the process.

Greg McDillon was the director of the Federal Air Marshal Program. He was promoted after being a FAM himself. Greg was stationed overseas for a number of years as a representative for the FAA in Germany. It was great to have him back stateside. He was a no nonsense, take no names kind of guy. I admired him a great deal. It was nice to have a straight shooter in the organization--especially so high up in management.

Greg prided himself on being the best and he wanted the best of the best as FAM's - best shooters, best physical shape, and best mental agility. Like I said he was a no nonsense kind of guy. Craig looked like he was in good physical condition, but I had no idea how well he shot a firearm. He was very enthusiastic about getting into the FAM program. I was hoping that he'd have the opportunity.

Since the program had become a voluntary program and the FAMS were based in Atlantic City, New Jersey, the requests from the existing special agent cadre had dwindled, at least here in the Western-Pacific Region. This was the first request I had gotten as deputy division manager so I was glad that I could call Greg personally with any questions I had.

When I turned away from my computer I saw the yellow memorandums of call slip sitting on the floor after being pushed under my closed door. I walked over, picked it up and smiled. It was a note from my daughter letting me know that she had gotten a "C" on her biology test.

That's my girl. Way to go, Monica.

. . .

Damn it, not again," I said, slamming down the phone. I raced out the door, hollering at Don Harding to follow me as I passed his office.

"We got another bird in the water," I said as I turned on the television.

"Who is it?"

We stood quietly and watched the local news channel for a few minutes. The reporter explained that Alaska Airlines flight 261 had crashed offshore about two miles north of Anacapa Island, here in California.

The map on the TV screen showed that Anacapa Island was off the central California coast near Port Hueneme in Ventura County. The island was actually composed of three volcanic islets that were part of the Channel Islands National Park.

The pilots had reported problems with their flight controls and needed to divert from landing at San Francisco International Airport to make an emergency landing at Los Angeles International Airport. But the flight never made it to the airport.

I called Luz and put her on speaker phone. The conference room fluorescent lights were flickering, doing a dull yellow dance throughout the room, as people slowly drifted into the room to watch the events unfold.

Most of our agents had gone home for the day, but a few of them worked until 5:00 P.M. and the division's secretary was still there.

"Maggie, I've got Rich Gordon and Roberta Packard responding to the airport now. We'll see what they can find out. And I've got a call in to Agent Stanton too."

"Okay, keep us posted, Luz."

The news was reporting that a commuter flight saw the aircraft roll over and plunge into the ocean at around 4:20 P.M.

"JJ, this is Maggie. Any idea how many people or crew were onboard the Alaska flight?"

"I'm still waiting for that information."

"Okay, and JJ find Cal Yates at the SFO CASFO for me please."

"Will do."

"Thanks."

Fifteen minutes later I had Cal on speaker phone. "Cal, have you heard about Alaska Air 261?"

"Yes and I'm headed back to the airport. Joe Muppett, SFO FSM, is already there. Alaska Air and airport officials are starting to set-up the VIP conference room so the people waiting for passengers on the flight have somewhere to go."

"Good. Any media calls yet?"

"Tons Maggie, but we'll handle it. The airport and the FAA public affairs office are talking to one another. So we'll keep you posted on what's going on."

"Thanks, Cal. We're on extension 3705 here in the conference room."

I hit the receiver button on the ringing conference room phone, and heard JJ say, "I'm connecting you with George Peters, Maggie."

"Maggie Stewart, Western-Pacific Region," I said when I heard Division Manager George Peters, come on the line from his Seattle, Washington office. He was a commanding presence even through the telephone wires. I could hear and feel his confidence and power ripple through the line as his voice boomed with authority. He was tall, handsome, and had one hell of a temper to go along with his powerful voice. If you needed to get a job done, call George and he'd find a way to get it done.

George Peters was my boss's colleague. He was the division manager responsible for the Northwestern part of the United States. The Alaska Airlines corporate office was in Seattle, Washington, which was why the Northwest Region was involved in an accident that occurred in California.

"Maggie, I've got agents deploying to the Alaska Airlines corporate office now and we're requesting a passenger manifest and are checking on what, if any, cargo was onboard," he barked into the phone.

I advised George on what we were doing here in L.A. and gave him the telephone extension number so he could call back directly with any updates.

As the evening wore on the Washington Operations Center informed us that a National Transportation Safety Board (NTSB) 'go team' had been established and they were enroute to the crash site.

The press secretaries for the Department of Transportation (DOT), Federal Aviation Administration (FAA), the Los Angeles Airport public affairs office, and Alaska Airlines were coordinating press releases and new conference updates.

"Guess you can tell I'm going to be late again, Monica," I said when I stepped into my office and quickly made a call home. "I've got some money on my dresser if you want to get take-out."

"Thanks, Mom. Mike and I will figure something out."

"Sorry honey. Great job on your biology test BTW."

"Thanks, Mom."

"I love you."

"Love you too. See you later."

Shaking off my melancholy mood I walked back into the conference room.

"Rich Gordon called in to let us know that the American Red Cross was setting up a station at LAX since about a half a dozen family members of some of the crew were showing up."

"Don Harding," he said when he picked up the conference room's ringing telephone. "Okay, thanks for the update, JJ."

Don turned and said, "Ron Pope called at the request of George Peters to let us know that there's an unconfirmed rumor that the Assistant U.S. Attorney's parents may have been on the flight."

"Sorry to hear that. But that will speed up the response team and heighten the political aspects of who's going to get involved now," I said with a slight bitter tone.

"It always does, Maggie, so let's see how this all plays out."

. . .

The following morning we learned that eighty-eight people had died - five crew members and eighty-three passengers, with at least thirty-five of them being connected to Alaska Airlines or Alaska's sister airline, Horizon Air. The Assistant U.S. Attorney's parents were not onboard.

Several pilots flying other aircraft saw Alaska Air 261 crash into the ocean; one pilot radioed: "That plane has just started to do a big huge plunge." The voice echoing from the television was filled with breaks in his voice. You could hear and feel the sadness, its dark tentacles strangling the room with despair.

Later when the Federal Bureau of Investigation (FBI), National Transportation Safety Board (NTSB), and Office of Inspector General (OIG) arrived there wasn't much more anyone could do. Alaska Airlines in Seattle was slow in responding to the FAA's request for the passenger manifest.

Finally, after multiple telephone calls, several from George, one of the FAA special agents based in Seattle drove over to Alaska's corporate office and retrieved a manifest.

. . .

"Let me walk you downstairs to John Clark's office," I said. "He's the manager for the Air Traffic Division. He'll get you a copy of the transcript for the last radio transmissions for the flight."

"Thanks, Maggie," Alan Friedman from the NTSB said.

Once the introductions were made between John Clark and Alan Friedman we all shook hands.

"Let me know if you need anything," I said.

"We will. And I'll make sure he gets escorted out of the building too," John said.

"Thanks. It was nice to meet you, Alan."

CHAPTER 14

Office Madness

"Well Maggie, it's been one heck of a month hasn't' it?" Tom said.

"It sure has. What a way to start a new year."

Nodding in agreement I began telling Tom the rest of the Monday morning news. "We've got some tough internal problems going on too. Linda just told me that all permanent change of station (PCS) moves have been put on hold because of the budget freeze. Emily's Performance Description (PD) got cancelled because of the freeze, so we probably won't be able to combine Charmaine and Marilyn's jobs – meaning we can't give Charmaine a pay increase. And we probably won't be able to get Marilyn into personnel security as a specialist either. Linda only had doom and gloom for me when she briefed me this morning. No good news at all, Tom. So, so much for trying to be efficient with our staffing levels, our budget is stagnant for the rest of this fiscal year."

"The budget under this current administration has been rough and I don't imagine it's going to get any better."

"I don't think so either after talking with Linda this morning," I replied.

"Close that door for me," Tom said with a head nod toward the open door.

After closing the door I settled back down on the black leather sofa that faced Tom's desk. When managers' doors get closed, the conversation about to commence isn't good.

"I received an email from Mike O. last week and the content was reported to the accountability board in D.C. Bruce called me about it this morning. Before I begin, Bruce's explicit instructions for you and me, is that we, and I quote, 'back away as far as we can from this issue and let the process take its course'."

"Okay, what happened?"

"The email I received stated that the Federal Security Manager (FSM) in San Francisco (SFO) was telling sex stories to two of the CASFO field agents. This conversation was overheard by another employee and reported to the CASFO manager in SFO. The manager reported it to the sexual harassment accountability board in Washington, D.C."

I began to fume. *I was certainly glad he bothered to call his boss first before he called D.C.*

Tom continued, "Bruce is in the hot seat as the accountability board official. And he is mandated to set up an investigation about the allegations. D.C. is involved now because, as you know, FSMs report to Washington, not us."

"Does the FSM know yet?"

"Probably, his boss was supposed to call first thing this morning. And Don Fairchild is flying out from Washington ASAP."

"We'll let this one play out, Maggie. We've got no control over the outcome, but I want to know why Cal didn't call us first before he called D.C. I'm not happy about getting blindsided."

"I don't know but I'll find out. Even if he called us after he called the accountability board, it would have been better," I said. I could feel my face reddening with frustration. *Here we go again between those two; Yates and Muppett are always at each other's throats.*

. . .

I finished my conversation with Cal by saying, "Cal, I understand the urgency of reporting quickly to the accountability board, but when you didn't at least give me a heads-up that an event got reported, you put Tom in a very bad position with D.C. And when Tom's in trouble I'm eventually in trouble too. You know Bruce was livid when he called Tom. Not because of the issue, but because Tom didn't know anything about it. That left Tom looking like he didn't know what was going on in his region."

"I did what I needed to do, Maggie. And I see now that I could have called you after I made the call. I felt like I was protecting my agents who are on the receiving end of the harassment."

"I understand that. But I have to say I think you were trying to get back at Joe too. I know you two don't get along."

"I disagree. We are very professional at all times."

"Okay, let's save this conversation for another time. For now understand that a heads-up on sensitive issues that may or may not get my boss in trouble, and me would be very much appreciated from now on. Understood?"

"Yes, Maggie."

"Thanks. Talk to you later."

I desperately needed some fresh air. I grabbed my jacket, keys, and sprinted down the six flights of stairs, skipping along as quickly as I could to get out of the building. I briskly walked past the security guard and out into the employee parking lot on the east side of the building.

On more than one occasion when I needed to clear my mind, solve a problem, or just escape from the stuffy office I'd walk around the federal building. Just a few loops through the parking lot, and then along the grass strip on the south side of the building, sidewalk, grass, and back into the parking lot. The constant drone of cars from the nearby 405 freeway and the cars on Aviation and Marina hummed in the back of my mind to remind me that I was in the city—but at least I was outside.

Cal and Joe had been disagreeing with each other for years. But it was a personality clash I could not get a handle on. Both men had enormous egos; Cal was politically connected, could get things done with a phone call, and always went the extra mile to support his friends, and quietly sabotage his enemies. He was a man you wanted on your team.

Joe, on the other hand, thought he was politically connected, but he wasn't. He was pompous, always telling everyone how great he was, and, that if he ever wanted to move to Washington, he'd have a job. Washington was always sending him out on 'special assessments' or 'overseas details' that carried a high profile. D.C. loved him – but most of the local staff didn't.

Joe had been a FAM too. We'd flown together a few times back in the FAM days. His large ego accompanied him wherever he went. Having an ego, especially in law enforcement, sometimes came with being a good agent. But there's a difference between a strong ego and a self-righteous ego.

Walking back to my office I wondered if anything would happen. *Maybe we'd get lucky on this one and he'd get transferred.* I crossed my fingers for luck.

. . .

Stanton walked into my office. "Where did spring go? Summer is about here. The kids are almost out of school?"

"I know, Maggie. This year is flying by."

"Any summer plans," I asked.

"Funny you should ask. I've just resigned!"

"What?"

"Yes, effective June first."

"No, tell me you're kidding, right?"

"I've been pretty frustrated with the direction of the FSM Program. I can't get any additional support, no funding, not even a secretary. Every time an incident occurs here I get the fallout. And when I remind headquarters that I need staff--if only just one administrative person to help me with the work load--I don't get any support."

I shook my head in disbelief.

"I'm starting a Hazmat Training Company. A woman named Pearl Billman is working with me. We're launching in July, Maggie."

"I still can't believe it. I don't want to believe it. What is the FAA going to do without you?"

"They'll be okay – you'll see."

"It will never be the same. You're my buddy, my partner in crime, and the smartest guy I know."

Several hours later, at home, pouring a glass of chardonnay, sitting outside in my small backyard, I cried. Huge sobs. *Nothing would be the same,* nothing.

And it wasn't the same. Within a month of Agent Stanton's departure, new introductions were made all around. "Luz, this is Ginny Hartman, the newly appointed federal security manager for LAX," I said. "Ginny, this is Luz Pase," the manager for the Los Angeles Civil Aviation Security Field Office.

"I'm glad you're here. You're definitely not in Kansas anymore," I said with a smile. It didn't take me long to realize my little joke fell on deaf ears. Ginny Hartman had transferred here from Kansas City but she didn't find any humor in my comment.

. . .

By the first of October I finished up the final review for the post of duty (POD) offices in San Diego and Sacramento. Tom and I were growing concerned that we didn't have an FAA presence at those two locations. Airline and cargo flights were on the increase. Our agents' travel cost and stay at those locations was on the rise too. It was time for us to station agents full-time at those locations. But doing so was a surprisingly bigger job. Job descriptions, pay grades, office space all needed to be approved by D.C. It took months and months of work and coordination.

Now it was almost done. Maybe we'd get this done by the end of the fiscal year. I hit the send button. *It all depended on end of year funding now.* I wanted Linda to look over the budget request one more time before I sent it to headquarters for review and hopefully their approval.

. . .

Tom glanced at me as I entered his office. "Maggie, I need you to go to Australia and meet with the CASLO there, Don Silverman. I'd go but I've got a two week detail as acting ACO-1, in D.C., so I need you to go."

"What's going on?"

"We have some high profile vendors traveling there in September and Don asked if we'd send regional management, the highest level we could, to assist with finalizing the coordination of meeting with these vendors. Mainly to show the airline folks there how important this passenger and baggage screening project is to the FAA. There's push-back from the industry because of cost and staffing issues. So it's a sensitive project and close to being derailed."

Looking at my planner, I said, "How about if I plan to leave at the end of next week? That will give me enough time for D.C. to give me a travel authorization, and make travel arrangements."

"Excellent. Thanks, Maggie."

Don Silverman met my flight when it arrived in Sydney the second week of May. He expedited my customs clearance and we were off and running. For the next two weeks, I visited three cities and two countries. I barely had time to eat or sleep, much less see any of the local sites.

"Don, are we done?" I said ten days into the trip. "If I don't bring something home for my kids I'm dead," I panned with a sad look on my face.

"I'm sorry, Maggie. I just wanted you to meet as many people as we could. Let's call it a day after lunch?"

"Wonderful. Thank you."

A few hours later, sitting in my hotel room, I was happy. *Monica was going to love the necklace I got her and Mike the wood carving of a turtle.* I opened my suitcase and began packing.

I was looking forward to going to New Zealand, I had heard so much about the country. We would spend three days in Auckland

and two days in Christ Church. I didn't know anything about Christ Church except that it was the capitol of New Zealand.

"Hello," I said, picking up the telephone in my room.

"Hi Mom, its Monica."

"Hey, how are you? Is everything okay? Is Mike okay?"

"Yes, we're fine, but I need to tell you something."

"You're pregnant!"

"Oh my God, how did you guess, Mom?"

"I'm a Mom and it's Mother's Day… somehow I just knew, honey. Need to talk?"

"No, the rest can wait until you come home. I just needed to tell you that I'm due in November."

I had a million thoughts, emotions, and questions but all I could say was, "I love you, girl. It will be okay, honey. Somehow, someway it will be okay."

Damn travel. I should be home now.

Don and I met almost as many people in New Zealand as we did in Australia. There was no down time except to eat and sleep. Finding time to go for a run was impossible.

Don waved to me as I boarded the New Zealand flight back to Los Angeles. I felt like I had been put through a washing machine, one cycle too many, on the hot water setting, and extra spins. What a whirlwind of a trip. And all in the name of coordination and diplomacy.

When I landed at LAX I felt a combination of exhaustion and elation. Elated to be home, to see my daughter, to talk about my future grandchild, and to sleep in my own bed.

. . .

The next three months were chaos at home and work. In the fall, Manhattan Beach High School, where Monica was a senior, refused to let her attend school because of 'safety and welfare' issues for the approaching baby.

"That's a bunch of B.S. and you know it," I angrily told the principal on the phone after Monica told me she was no longer able to attend school.

Monica tried to calm me down. "At least they are going to let me walk at graduation next year, Mom. And I can go to the prom too."

"Well, well how kind of the snobby Manhattan Beach School District to let you walk with them. What a crock."

"It is what it is. They gave me the address of the alternative school in Torrance where I can go. I'll drive over there tomorrow and check it out."

"Okay honey. We don't have a choice, do we?"

"Nope."

. . .

I was up, barely. I answered the phone in my upstairs bedroom.

"Maggie, its Cal. Have you seen what's happening?

"No."

"Turn on the TV," he said. "It's not good."

CHAPTER 15

Nineteen Madmen Strike

I didn't have a TV upstairs so I raced downstairs, clicked on the remote, turned on the coffee pot, and watched the TV crackle and come to life. As I stood staring in disbelief, I glimpsed black, thick, billowing smoke floating out of a tall building into the clear, blue skyline of New York City. I recognized the building.

The house phone rang again.

I grabbed it after the first ring, "Hello?"

"Maggie, Tom. Are you aware of what's going on?"

"Cal called. I just turned on the TV. It's horrible. I can't believe what I'm seeing."

"The World Trade Center has been hit by an airplane. Very, very preliminary information is coming in. The FAA was notified at 8:32 this morning, east coast time that an American Airlines flight was hijacked after departing from Boston. A national telecom is scheduled to begin in thirty minutes. I'm on my way into the office now."

"Roger that. I'll head there too."

"We're standing up the regional command center. See you at the office," and the line went dead as Tom hung up.

I had taken the day off work to have the carpets cleaned. Sandee wagged her tail, hoping I was going to let her outside.

I stood staring at the TV; shock, disbelief, and confusion filled my thoughts as I saw fire shooting out the sides of the World Trade Center. I felt numb. The minutes ticked on and CNN kept showing more and more images of death and destruction; destruction caused by an airplane crashing into the World Trade Center. *This couldn't be happening.*

Minutes later another airplane crashed into the second tower.

"God! Oh God, no!" To my horror I saw people, tiny black objects falling to the earth – The news announcer's voice was shaking with emotion.

I couldn't believe my eyes. I felt a growing sense of anger and profound sadness. And fear. Images of fire, black smoke, hell on earth, filled the television screen.

I wanted to touch my kids. I knew they were safe, but I wanted to physically see them, hug them, and hear their voices. It would be easy to hug Monica since she was upstairs fast asleep in her bed.

Hugging Mike wouldn't be so easy. He decided, last month, after having a fabulous vacation with his Dad, to move to Greece. His Dad had been living there for about a year. His decision was really tough for me, but I knew if I didn't let him go he'd always hold it against me.

I knew all about holding a grudge. When I was a sophomore in high school my best friend, Ruthy Globus, was moving to Germany for a year with her family. I was invited to go along – I wanted to – but my Dad said no. I was devastated. I remember as if it was yesterday. I was so angry at my Dad. It was a missed opportunity. And I wasn't going to see my best friend for a year. Who was I going to hang out with? When this opportunity came along for Mike, well, I couldn't say no.

Call Mikey later, Maggie. He's okay. At least he's out of the country. No telling what's going on here. I raced upstairs to change clothes and to hug my daughter.

Kneeling beside Monica's bed, I touched the top of her head, kissed her cheek, and whispered, "Gotta go to work, kiddo. Love you."

Sleepily Monica said, "Love you too, Mom. Bye."

. . .

At the office, standing in the conference room--several of us with our arms crossed tightly against our chests, some with a hand covering their mouth, some with hands balled into fists--not a word was spoken. We were joined in solidarity as we silently watched the horrific events unfold, the telephone lines from the national telecom clicked, cracked, and clattered away from one end of the country to the other. Occasionally someone would call out 'open mike' to advise someone that the discussions they were having in their office or conference room could be heard by everyone else in the country.

"Attention everyone on this line, as of 0940 hours, Jane Garvey, FAA administrator has just ordered every U.S. aircraft to land ASAP. We're shutting down the entire United States air traffic system."

The conference call exploded into conversations punctuated with shock, disbelief, and anguish. Everyone wanted more information.

Tom said, "Don, I want every agent called in to work ASAP. We're going to need agents at every airport."

"We've activated the phone tree, Tom. We're calling in everyone now," Don Harding said.

"Maggie, I want you to find the LAX Federal Security Manager Ginny Hartman. Find Luz too. Make sure Luz and her agents from the LAX Field Office are available to assist Ginny in anything she needs at LAX."

"Yes, sir."

"One more thing – plan on taking the swing shift here and I'll cover the day shift. We'll tag team the command center for now."

"Got it."

The next several hours were filled with telecom after telecom. The five field office managers sent every available agent to their airports from Hawaii to Nevada. Knowing it would take several hours to get every agent in place, I decided to leave the office and run home to check on Monica, grab a bag, and head back to the office.

I quickly drove down Aviation Boulevard to my house, which was less than a mile away.

"Hi honey," I said to Monica when I got home.

"Hi, Mom. This is so scary," she said as she nodded her head in the direction of the TV.

"It is. I'm not sure what we're up against, but I'm going to leave you money so you don't go hungry. I'm going to be at the office 24/7 for the next few days anyway."

"Alright. I'll be okay."

"I know, honey. You are very self-sufficient for being a senior in high school. But call Brenda if you need anything. I'll call her now and let her know I might be at the office for a few days….and nights."

Taking the steps two at a time, I grabbed my black canvas travel bag, and quickly packed toiletry items and a few extra clothes. The uncertainty of what lay ahead was nerve wracking to say the least so I tried to prepare as best I could.

. . .

"It's eerie," I said to Agent Hartman as I stood in her office on Wednesday, September 12th.

"Yes, it's very strange."

Several of the agents assigned to the LAX CASFO gathered at Hartman's office for the 6:00 A.M. morning briefing. I drove over from the regional office to see how things were going.

After showing my credentials to gain access to the airport, I parked my drab, dusty gray g-car in the adjacent parking lot next to what we called the 'theme' building. It was the Jettison space ship cartoon-like structure in the center of LAX Airport and Lee's office was at the base of that building.

With every aircraft in the United States grounded, the only noise you heard at the airport was the announcement "parking is restricted except in designated white zone."

"I never heard those announcements before, and I sure wish I wasn't hearing them now," I said to no one in particular.

"The National Guard has been called upon to augment security at every U.S. airport in the country."

"A National Guard liaison from Van Nuys, California will be at the regional office later this afternoon. They will have someone assigned 24/7 in our command center to coordinate their guard operation with every field office manager and federal security manager in the region."

"I'm heading back to my office, Ginny," I said. "I'll catch up with you later. I've got another telecom in about an hour."

The 7:00 A.M. telecom was my second one of the day.

When Washington, D.C. asked about agent deployments across the country, Don Harding reported, "Affirmative, we have agents at every airport except a couple of airports in Hawaii. With the aviation system shut-down we couldn't fly anyone from Honolulu to Maui or Kona."

. . .

Dialing into the telecom at 2:00 P.M. I listened as various phone lines connecting the country's security network came to life. I heard familiar voices from all nine regions from Alaska to New York.

"Western-Pacific Region," the operations specialist from Washington, D.C. called out.

"Tom Thomas and Maggie Stewart," Tom said for both of us in an attempt to save time.

"Hi everyone, this is Lynn. Thanks for responding so quickly," she said. "I am going to get right to the point. Effective immediately I have been asked by Jane Garvey, our FAA Administrator to accept a 'special detail' involving this attack for an unspecified amount of time. I will be leaving FAA Security at the end of the week to accept this detail. Therefore, effective immediately Steven House will become ACO-1, Pat Dee, ACI-1, Lee Levi, ACP-1, and Max Paper, ACP-2."

Lynn went on to say, "Since the 9/11 attacks, every flight in the

U.S. is grounded. We're at war now so to speak. We've been attacked, now we're in this for the long run, and we need to do our jobs differently. Everything is going to be different from the way we operated before - at airports, airlines, ground operations, and cargo - every facet of aviation. We're going to regulate every segment of aviation – areas that we never regulated before."

"The air marshal program has been authorized to hire five to six hundred agents. We're targeting former military and law enforcement – the best-of-the-best to defend this country. The hiring process will be massive. We are depending on every region to give us resources when we need them. I know everyone is already running thin; however, President Bush requested that we have an air marshal on every international and domestic flight." Pausing to take a breath she then said, "We took a hit and now it's time to counter-attack."

You could hear the cheers on every telecom across the country.

"Finally, I'm going to be working directly for Jane Garvey. I'll be going over to the DOT Building starting tomorrow morning. I'm going to help bring all of the organizations within the FAA together, assist in making some short and long term recommendations to a Blue Ribbon team established by Secretary Minetta. The FAA is going to assist getting the airline industry back up and flying full force again and make sure that this never ever happens again."

Enthusiastic cheers and applause followed Lynn's statement.

"Now I'm going to hand this telecom over to Steven," she said. I could hear her chair squeak as I pictured her turning to Steven House. "And one more thing, I'm personally asking each and every one of you to support this new team."

"Thank you, Lynn. We will miss you here in ACS but we know you're needed more where you're going."

"So here's what I need from every manager here in headquarters and for all of you folks out in the field. It's not just Ramsey Yousef anymore. As you know now it's a whole different threat. The threat isn't limited to the airside, but to every part of aviation security. There will be physical security changes, personnel security changes, which means more security directives, and more emergency amendments. So work with headquarters on this. We don't have a timeline, we will make changes as we deem necessary. This is not the time to slow down. We are going to need additional support in D.C. We will ask the field for those resources."

Steven took a breath and continued, "It's time to transition from crisis to long haul planning. If you aren't already doing it, document what you are doing. Write everything down. If you have questions, send them here. We're establishing a focal point for all and any operational questions here in ACO. This is not the time to 'wing it' folks. If in doubt, ask. Now get organized and get rested. Remember we're in this for the long haul now."

"Let's start answering questions. I'm going to call out each region starting on the West Coast with Tom. Tom? Questions?"

After two hours of conversation, Steven wrapped up the telecom, "Remember the Security Directives [SDs] are probably going to continue to come out daily. We're all going to be very, very busy for a very long time. I expect everyone to use good judgment. As we finalize the hiring plans we'll get them out to each division manager as quickly as we can. We're getting direct hire authority for temporary and contract employees. Keep up the good work everyone. Washington out."

. . .

In the days ahead every manager, supervisor, special agent, and staff support personnel worked twelve hour shifts, seven days a week. Tom was the incident command manager from 6:00 A.M. to 6:00 P.M. and I was officially on duty from 6:00 P.M. to 6:00 A.M. In reality, we were in the office 24/7, napping when we could, where we could. We were running on adrenaline, coffee, and anger.

Washington held telecoms daily at 6:00 A.M. and 2:00 P.M. to brief the field on the constant changes that were occurring. The number of briefings, security directive changes, and press attention was staggering.

"Good morning, everyone," Steven said. "We've got a lot of information to pass along to you folks today."

In the background, someone in D.C. cleared their throat as papers rustled, and pens clicked in anticipation of the update to follow.

"Effective immediately the government will begin having federal oversight at the airport screening checkpoints. A government contract workforce will be established, supervised by the government to ensure command, control, and consistency in screening passengers and carry-on items. We've been given 500 million dollars in funding."

Steven continued, "The National Guard will remain at U.S. airports until this oversight is fully in place. The air marshal program is being significantly ramped up – there's a separate telecom in about an hour to discuss that."

"The Hill is demanding competent leadership at all levels. We are faced with a cunning and dedicated enemy now. We can no longer afford weaknesses in any part of our organization. Each one of you needs to understand that our sense of purpose is security. Tighter security than it's ever been before. Our organizational mission has not changed, but the way we do business and our partnerships have changed significantly."

"One more comment before I go. We all have jobs so don't worry. Just remember my expectation and the American people's expectation is that each one of you continue to lead by example. Use good judgment in everything you do. Bob Builder will manage the rest of this telecom for me now. I'm heading over to the DOT Building to meet with Lynn."

"Good afternoon...."

. . .

After the national telecoms each regional office held local telecoms to redistribute staffing or provide clarification to the field offices and agents about the fluid work world we were all swimming in.

"We're connected and standing by for the FAM telecom, Tom," I said with the mute button on.

"Thanks, Maggie."

The 1:00 P.M. telecom clicked to life and Greg began outlining the intense but stringent hiring process that was being organized for the first time in the history of the FAA. Assessment centers were being established in New Jersey, Atlanta, Dallas, Seattle and Los Angeles.

"It's about the massive hiring President Bush has mandated. The president wants air marshals on every U.S. flight. ASAP," Greg Mc Dillon explained. "We've been given authorization to hire six hundred additional marshals." The tough part for Greg and the agency was that it had to be done within 30 days!

Greg explained, "This is a pass or fail, eight hour process, folks, for these applicants. The interview, firearms qualification, medical, psychological, drug, and agility testing will all take place at one of the assessment centers we are starting up."

Greg continued, "We plan to interview 125 applicants per day throughout the country. This means each assessment facility must process twenty-five people per day. The center will be open for one week." Pausing again, I could hear Greg taking a sip of something, he went on to say, "If the applicant successfully passes each phase, they will be given an offer letter at the end of the day." The number of briefings, security directive changes, and press attention was overwhelming.

"Does the offer letter mean they are hired," someone asked.

"Tentatively, yes. But they must still pass the training course and a full background check for their security clearance."

. . .

"Mom, my water broke."

"On my way."

I raced out the door, trotted down six flights of stairs, jumped in my car, peeled out of the parking lot, onto Marine Avenue, then Aviation Boulevard. I was home in less than ten minutes.

"I'm going to drive myself to the hospital. It's not that far away," Monica said to me from behind the wheel of her green Ford Bronco.

"No, no I want to go with you."

"It's okay, Mom. I got this." Starting her car, while it sat in neutral idling for a minute, she put her elbow on the window frame, cupped her chin in her hand, looked at me and smiled – a lips-closed, no-teeth smile, but the look of determination and strength was shining in her eyes.

Okay. Okay. Okay, but I didn't like this. However, I said, "I love you. I'll follow you – okay?" I said as I patted her hand and kissed her on the cheek.

Like my son, Mike, my daughter Monica was a strong, fiercely independent, and confident person. I didn't want her to drive herself, but I knew by the look on her face, that determination, that she in fact was going to do exactly what she needed to do.

No sense wasting any more time. First babies took forever anyway, but just in case this baby didn't wait I needed to get a move on.

Seven hours later my first grandchild, Amber, arrived, greeting her mom with a healthy yell.

. . .

"Stewart here," I said grabbing the ringing telephone on my desk, as I briskly walked into my office – later than usual.

"Maggie, this is Pete Flint. We've got a situation at LAX. I just got off the telephone with the LAX police chief."

Puzzled, I said, "Okay."

"Apparently the federal security manager has barricaded herself in her office. She won't come out."

"What?"

"I'm going to catch the first flight I can. But for now I need you to get to the airport and find out what's happening."

"I'm on my way now."

CHAPTER 16

Back on Watch

"You can see her there. Look, Lieutenant McRoy said, pointing. "She's under the desk?"

Cupping my hands on the glass front door, pressing my face into my hands,

I looked through the glass into the federal security manager's office. I did indeed see a figure crouched under a desk.

Knocking, he said, "Lieutenant McRoy, airport police, we need to speak with you, Ms. Hartman."

No response.

"Do you have a key?" McRoy asked.

"No, I don't."

"We may have to call airport maintenance out here."

"Let's try again. Maybe between the two of us we can coax her out."

Gently tapping on the glass, "Ms. Hartman, Ginny, its Maggie. Can you open the door for me?"

"No, go away."

The knock was louder and firmer this time. Tapping on the glass, I could feel my knuckles rubbing against the Federal Aviation Administration logo that was embossed on the door, I said, "Come on, girl. It will be okay. You've had a lot on your plate."

Tapping a little harder, "We're here to take some of the burden off you. I'm so, so sorry you've been under so much pressure."

Fifteen minutes turned into thirty minutes but eventually she crawled out from under her desk and unlocked the office door.

"It will be okay. It's going to be okay, Ginny. Let's go get some fresh air," I said as we slowly walked away from her office.

By then a few more police officers, an ambulance, and a paramedic had responded.

"The main thing is she's safe, Tom. And, thank God, no press. Pete will be here late this afternoon. We'll figure out a game plan then."

"Okay, Maggie. Great job – thanks."

Hanging up the phone, I said, "Okay, now what?" I could feel the weight of the world upon my shoulders. I was exhausted. We all were. I never saw this coming.

. . .

I walked toward Pete when I saw him come out of the jetway and into the American Airlines terminal.

Walking through the terminal was unsettling me. "I can't believe the National Guard is here. It's been quite an adjustment," I said to Pete.

"Airports have changed dramatically in a very short time period haven't they?" he said.

"National Guard, no one beyond screening, expect paying passengers, no press, secondary screening at every gate, I'd say."

"Our way of doing business will never be the same."

From Terminal 4, the walk to the FSM's office took about ten minutes.

"I had the airport cleaning staff come out and clean the office up a bit, Pete. This place smelled pretty bad. She'd been in there awhile."

"Can you tell me what happened?"

"I'm not sure. Ginny and Luz are in direct communication more than I am. You should probably talk with Luz too. But I think Ginny had too much on her plate. You know, LAX is huge. She's been running full speed, like all of us, since nine eleven without the benefit of knowing the airport like the back of her hand. You know, like Stanton did. She didn't have enough time to learn everything."

"Yes, the FAA has been going ballistic trying to meet all of the demands being placed on us by Department of Transportation, Office of Management and Budget, the National Security Council, the White House Staff, not to mention the House and Senate Congressional committees."

"She wasn't here very long before nine eleven happened. She was on a major learning curve; airport layout, airlines, station managers, airport management, and us – she didn't know the FAA agents here very well either. Just too much too fast."

"I understand."

"And the changes are coming in daily. Heck. Hourly. The FSM is where the buck stops at the Category X airports."

Pete nodded.

"To add to the workload, every legislator, politician, and journalist is out here trying to get face time on the evening news. People are stalking you and staking out this airport. And who do they want to be seen with? The highest FAA aviation security official at the airport."

"Ginny, the FSM," Pete said, finishing my sentence.

"She crashed. Too much, too fast, and sadly not enough help."

"I'll make sure she has some help now," Pete said. "In fact, rest assured I'll make sure my team gets the resources they need."

. . .

"Hey there. Good to see you. So, you're no longer a vampire," Agent Stanton said looking at his watch, noting it was 9:00 A.M. "I heard you've been on the swing shift since nine eleven."

"YES! You're back," I said as I ran over and gave him a huge hug, squeezing him as tight as I could. "Every shift actually. And you're not a ghost either."

Looking over at Pete I said, "You said you'd get resources to your FSM team – well, you weren't kidding. John Wayne here, I mean

Agent Stanton, is the best-of-the-best. We're all going to benefit by having him back."

"You should have been at the airport police meeting earlier this morning. The PD here is jumping up and down. They were screaming about the press trying to get through security."

"You would have loved it," Stanton said, grinning from ear to ear.

"Everyone at the meeting was talking, arguing, and looking for solutions on how to solve the press demanding they get access through the checkpoints when they aren't ticketed passengers," Pete said.

"They all kept arguing until somebody figured out I was in the room."

"They all stopped talking, and the station manager for United looked at Stanton. He asked what he thought."

"I took the pressure out of the room and told everyone that the press better have a ticket or they don't get in."

"So you're the FSM at LAX effective midnight last night, right?"

"Yes, I'm getting an administrative assistant too," Stanton said, positively glowing.

"We finally got additional funding for our FSMs," Pete said matter-of-factly.

"So after everyone knew I was back on the job they chuckled, relaxed a little bit, and we all went back to work. It feels like I haven't been gone long at all. My phone started ringing like crazy all over again."

"Thank goodness, you're back. It's been almost three weeks, eighteen days to be exact. But who's counting! I for one am totally relieved to see you again, my friend."

"And with that – it's time for me to catch my flight," Pete announced.

"And I need to get back to the office. I'm sure there's another emergency amendment or security directive that's in need of implementation," I said.

Pete, Lee and I all shook hands and I headed back to the office.

LAX was in good hands once again. Agent Stanton was back!

CHAPTER 17

Yes, More Changes

"Good news, thanks Chuck." Getting up from my chair I walked around the corner to Tom's office and popped my head in the door.

"I just got off the phone with Chuck Henry from flight standards and he confirmed that the Special Federal Air Regulation [SFAR] will be published tomorrow."

"Okay," said Tom, "send out an email to our managers and let them know."

Back at my desk I made a note so I wouldn't forget to send out the email Tom requested. I decided to send the email out after lunch just in case we had more changes or notifications.

The SFAR would add an additional requirement to keep cockpit doors locked at all times and decide who would have possession of door keys. Prior to 9.11 almost every crew member had a key or the door was locked only during takeoff or landing. Those rules were changing tomorrow, just a few weeks after 9.11.

The other issue that had impacted some airline or contract employees who worked as skycaps was coming to the surface too. Most of these people had been fired or no longer made the same amount of money because checking bags for any flight was no longer allowed.

One of our FAA security directives was responsible for that. An unintended consequence. There was a meeting at LAX Airport about it tonight at 6:00 P.M. but now that Agent Stanton was back I didn't need to attend.

The vendor issue was another problem. Gaining access into the secured areas, background checks, searching their inventory required additional security screening now too.

"Hi there. Checking in to see how it's going. Call when you get time.

Five seconds later my phone rang. "FAA Security, Agent Stewart."

"Hey there. I was on the other phone when you called," Agent Stanton said. "What's going on?"

"Just checking in since I haven't talked to you in a couple of days. There's a SFAR about cockpit door requirements coming out tomorrow that I wanted to make sure you knew about. And I wanted to see how the skycap and vendor issues are going there."

"With the security directives in place for curbside check-in restrictions and only ticketed passengers beyond the checkpoint there isn't really anything I can tell them that can help, Maggie. Biggest thing I'm going to do is listen."

"I know, the restrictions are causing a lot of havoc, that's for sure. We've really changed the way we're doing business at airports – couldn't be helped – tighter security now than ever."

"I just got off the phone with a very angry airline station manager because the airlines are complaining that the vendors can't service the airlines. In fact, my other phone is ringing again, Maggie. I'll call you later on. Bye"

"Bye."

"Maggie, the operations center just called to advise me that an American Airlines flight from Dallas Fort Worth on the way to Honolulu has been diverted to LAX because one of the flight attendants found a box cutter stashed in some dishes. Agent Hazen is responding to LAX now."

Okay, keep me posted. Call Stanton and tell him too just in case D.C. hasn't notified him yet."

"Will do," Don said.

Fifteen minutes later Don poked his head back in my office door. "American Airlines flight 5 landed at 10:50 A.M. Agent Hazen, Stanton, and the FBI are at the remote."
"Ok. Thanks, Don."

Thirty minutes later I got another call. "Maggie, Reno Tower just reported that something or someone parachuted and landed south of the Aero Creek Parkway near the airport. But the parachute was not fully opened. This information was reported to the tower by an anonymous caller who left a message on a recorded line."
"And..."
"The tower chief called the operations center to report the incident; he sounded spooked."
"Do we have anyone in Reno that can go take a look, Don?"
"I've got a call into Ron Fountain now. I'll let you know."

. . .

"Morning."
"Morning yourself," Stanton chimed back at me.
"How's it going here?" I said between sips of coffee. "There are so many things going on at once that it's impossible to keep up."
"I know. How's the hiring going?"
"Oh, that project," I said, shaking my head. "Well, from the hundred and thirty-seven temporary positions that were authorized by Office of Personnel Management [OPM] nationally. Western-Pacific Region got forty positions. The interviews, thankfully are done – and tentative offers have been sent out. This was a team effort without a doubt. Cecil, Dewanna, Garnetta, Linda, and Donna have been godsends in getting everything done. We all sat down this last weekend to figure out hiring criteria, pay banding, salary cap decision, and temporary security clearances."
"Now I'll have some help too."

"You sure will. And I think we'll be able to get these agents, rather Aviation Security Inspectors [ASIs] up and running pretty quick. Everyone we hired here in AWP worked for an airline previously. You know a lot of airline personnel got laid off after nine-eleven – with the flight schedules being reduced by almost a third, the airlines didn't need so many employees, so they terminated them. I've got to say we're happy to have them. We've got abbreviated one week training classes already scheduled in Oklahoma City for them too. I was exhausted but we got it done, Lee."

"It's a win for everyone. I'm glad to hear it," he said. "But you know we'll still need additional help. We've got more security directives and emergency amendments than we've ever had implemented at one time."

"I hear you."

. . .

Staggering through the front door after another twelve hour day, I heard my granddaughter crying, and I heard my daughter's feet walking across the wooden floor upstairs. Monica was walking in cadence with each of Amber's expressive wails of displeasure.

"Hi honey. I don't think I'll ask you how your day went," I said as I gently took Amber into my arms.

"She's so fussy, Mom. She's got gas big time," Monica exclaimed.

"Some babies are like that. I'm sorry she's so fussy. Hey, I'll take her for a walk. That might help. You always liked going on walks. Get me a bottle and we'll go for a stroll."

After bundling Miss Amber up, I grabbed my shoes and we were ready. "Where's her bottle, honey?"

"Here. Is there any chance you can watch her for a while tonight too? I want to hang out with a few of my friends later on."

"I can do that but don't stay out too late. I'm still in one hell of a mess at work – nine-eleven really changed the way we do business. Never, ever again are we going to take a hit like the one we did."

"I know, Mom. Thanks. I love you. I'll be home by ten P.M. – promise."

Amber settled down enough to let me put her in her stroller so we could walk the neighborhood. I walked down Durfour Street to Vail Avenue, south toward Artesia Boulevard. I loved these semi-quiet streets. We passed through the grassy park where my kids played not so long ago. The baseball fields were lit, and a few of the local ball clubs were practicing. Fond memories came flooding back as we walked by. I could tell by the loud voices, occasional cheers, and squeals that fun was being had by both sides. I welcomed the cool air, fresh and with a slight scent of the ocean which was about two miles away.

Walking Miss Amber was a marvelous escape from the horror, sadness, and continual stress since 9.11. The relentless changes, demands, and official inquiries from every agency that had a three letter acronym, (FBI, DOT, OMB, CIA), were endless. The request for documents and data flowed downhill – downhill to the agents working in the field. When we sent information to D.C., D.C. sent more requests. Everyone was going crazy trying to meet all of the demands placed upon every manager, supervisor, and agent in FAA Security.

We were briefed that Congress was forming an organization called the Transportation Security Administration (TSA) within the Department of Transportation (DOT) and that eventually our positions would be transferred from FAA into the newly formed TSA. That was the rumor on the street. Sooner-than-later, but eventually SF-52 would be created. Then, and only then, would our personnel transfers be official. For now, it was all just that – a rumor. But a frightening rumor.

I'd spent my entire career with the FAA. I loved the organization. I loved what I did for a living. I loved serving the aviation community. I wasn't sure what the future held but I knew for the time being I had to concentrate on the job at hand.

Remember your trade, your craft, Maggie, and you'll be okay. You're good at what you do.

As I turned the corner from Artesia onto Greenwood I looked down at my sleeping grandchild. I shuddered, hoping she'd always be as safe as she was right now. I felt alone; lonely at work, lonely at home, yet I was surrounded by people, activity, noise, and challenges. Aviation security was a lonely profession and 9.11 made it even lonelier.

. . .

"I'm home, Mom."

"Hi honey. Amber's been asleep since eight P.M. Apparently so have I," I said as I slowly got up from the sofa.

"Did you have a good time?"

"I did. We had a blast. Thanks."

"You're welcome. Love you. I'm off to bed."

"Night, Mom."

"Night."

CHAPTER 18

Alaska Bound

"You want me to go where?"

"Anchorage," Mary Connors said. I could picture her sitting at her desk in Washington, D.C., her plump shape covered by baggy clothes, her hair semi-unkempt, and her nails clipped short. She never looked like a Washingtonian. She always marched to her own drum when it came to fashion. We didn't ever underestimate her – she was a powerhouse in her own right. When it came to staunch loyalty to our ACS Director Steven House or knowing the FAA Human Resource rules and regulations, Maureen was the 'go to gal'.

"I've never considered living in Alaska," I said, trying to stall for time.

This call came completely out of the blue. What the heck was I going to say?

"Consider it, Maggie. We've got some personnel issues up there and we know you can straighten them out. George Peters has been up there for about six weeks as Acting -700 Division Manager, but he can't do that forever. We want you to be the permanent manager. I'll give you until tomorrow to decide."

"Okay, talk to you tomorrow, Mary. Thanks for the opportunity."

"Think hard on this," she said. This opportunity is a once-in-a-lifetime offer."

. . .

As promised, the next morning Mary called. "Well, what's your decision, Maggie?"

"I'm ready. I talked to my daughter and she said 'go-for-it'. So it looks like I'm moving to Anchorage."

"I'll call you later with all the details. Let me be the first to congratulate you."

. . .

Looking out the oval-shaped window, seat belt buckled for landing, I only saw snow as the landing lights passed the runway markers and we gently rolled onto the hard landing surface at the Anchorage Airport. Snow was piled everywhere, and was plowed off the active runways, taxiways, and access roads. There was more snow than I had ever seen. It was beautiful.

Looking at my watch, 5:00 P.M., *and it was pitch black.* I slowly inched my way up to the front of the aircraft. Every passenger standing in the aisle began gathering hats, scarves, coats, and thick gloves from the overhead bins above their seats. As they rolled or carried their carry-on luggage forward I smiled as I saw a sea of thick coats.

When I got to baggage claim I immediately saw George Peters. His white hair stood out like a beacon in a crowd of dark woolen-covered heads. "Welcome to Anchorage."

"Thank you, George. It's nice to see you again. It's freezing in here," I said as I pulled my coat tighter around me.

"Wait until you get outside. It's nineteen degrees. A warm, balmy day here," George Peters said with a sharp, loud laugh. "Hungry?"

"Yes, I'm starved and I'd love a glass of wine."

"I've got just the place – come on – let's go find my car."

Walking into the Glacier Brew House in downtown Anchorage I immediately felt warmer. "Two," George said to the hostess.

As we walked over to be seated I looked up at George and smiled. I could tell he was scanning the room for any potential problems. He was tall, fit, and striking. Both handsome, well groomed, and gave off a swashbuckling self-assurance that was very appealing. I immediately liked him. I immediately trusted him.

"What can I get you to drink?" the server asked.

"A glass of Chardonnay for me please," I said.

"And a Moosehead on tap for me," George said.

As we waited for our drinks I looked around. The restaurant and bar was cozy, inviting, and lovely. The open ceilings showed the heating and air conditioning system for the building, the floors were a hardy light brown wood, and there was an enormous fire burning in the fireplace centered in the middle of the restaurant.

My glass of chardonnay came promptly as did George's beer. We made small talk, looked at the menu, made our choices, and ordered.

"This is my favorite place to eat here in town," George told me.

"And it will be walking distance for you from your corporate apartment and the office. Dana Jersey, your administrative officer kept you within walking distance of everything. Just like you asked, Maggie."

"I can't wait to meet her. She sounded so nice when I talked to her on the phone."

"She's terrific. Great personality, strong work ethic, tempered with humor, compassion, and grit. I like her a lot."

"That's good to hear. If you like her, I like her," I said after taking a sip of my wine.

We both had lobster bisque and halibut for dinner.

"That was delicious. I will be here a lot, I suspect."

At the apartment complex I grabbed my bag from the backseat of George's car and thanked him for dinner.

"You are very welcome. I'll see you here at 7:30 A.M. It will be easier to pick you up since you need an Alaska Region identification badge to get into both the building and the parking garage. I'll escort you in tomorrow and then Dana can do the rest."

"Sounds like a plan. Thanks again. See you tomorrow."

. . .

The drive to the office was a few short blocks. The sidewalks were piled high with snow. It didn't look as magical as last night. It was still dark, but I could see the soot covering the snow piles as we drove by, the car jiggled as the tires rode across bumps of ice and snow. I'd never seen snow piled so high. In some places it was above my head.

"Morning, Fred," George said to the contact security guard at the entrance to the employee parking garage.

"Morning, George."

"We'll be getting Ms. Stewart a regional badge later this morning. She's the new division manager for security, AAL-700. Starts today."

"Well, welcome to Anchorage."

"Thanks Fred. I'm glad to be here."

Once we showed Fred our FAA Identification badges we were granted access into the garage.

Briskly walking through the garage toward the elevator banks I could feel the cold air touching my face, my fingers and my toes.

"I'm going shopping after work for warmer clothes I can tell you that already, George. This California girl didn't realize just how cold and dark it was going to be up here in January," I said as my teeth began to chatter.

"You'll get acclimated. It's a dry cold – trust me – you'll be out in shorts in no time!"

. . .

"Thanks for the lift to the airport, Maggie," George said two weeks later. "It's been a pleasure working with you. I'll arrange to get back up here for a visit in about six weeks."

"That would be great. I should have a lot of things straightened out by then, but I can always use a second pair of eyes."

I got back to the office in just enough time to dial into the Monday morning weekly telecom. As roll call was taken I quickly wrote down a few notes so I'd remember what I wanted to talk about when my name was called.

"There's two issues that need addressing immediately here. The first one is the antiquated computer system. We're still working off of T-One lines for our internet access and the rest of FAA Security is already on T-Three. We don't have an IT person here so I'd like to have our computer specialist from Western-Pacific Region come up and take a look at our system. I've spoken briefly to Tom about this and he's given his approval as long as D.C. will authorize the funding."

"Ok, we'll look into that and get back to you ASAP," Steven House said.

"The second issue I'm working on is the badging system. The badging system for the region is at the operations center not the security office. I'm getting significant push-back from the regional administrator [RA] to move the badging responsibilities back to our office and under our jurisdiction. I can't figure out how we lost control of it in the first place. Dana Jersey, our administrative assistant, has already agreed to manage the badging office once we have it moved back here. And I will be asking our personnel security specialists to assist too, that is, unless you can give me another full time employee [FTE]," I said with my fingers crossed.

I paused and then continued, "So if the RA calls you to protest and complain about what I'm doing I wanted you to have a heads-ups about it."

"Thanks, Maggie. I doubt that we can dedicate an FTE for you so I'm glad you've figured out a work-around for the problem. But I'll speak with Mary Connors about staffing a position there and maybe we can make that happen."

"Thanks, Steven. I don't have any other issues here."

. . .

A few weeks later Nelson Wick, the IT specialist I borrowed from

California arrived from Los Angeles with the same first impression that I had.

"It's freezing," he said as we hurried to my g-car that was parked just outside the baggage claim area.

"I know. But it's a spectacular place, Nelson. I love it here already."

As George Peters did for me, our first stop was the Glacier Brew House for dinner. He ordered halibut, me salmon and we feasted, chatted, and talked for nearly two hours about what needed to be done here for the internet systems. I dropped him off in front of the Hilton Hotel a few blocks away from the restaurant. "I hope you don't mind but can I come by and get you around nine? I have an early telecom at 6:30 A.M. and I'm not sure how long it will last. It's more news about our transition over to TSA. Besides sunrise is at 8:45 A.M. so you'll see Alaska – if you come in early you won't – our office is in the basement of the federal building. Daylight is a premium for us during the winter months," I said with a smile. "We still have about eight hours of daylight here."

"Oh, okay. I'll see you at nine tomorrow."

"Sounds good. Thanks for coming up, Nelson. We certainly need the help, plus it's good to see you."

. . .

At 6:30 A.M. the national telecom had just begun with its usual clicks and chimes as telephone lines across the country were connected into the secure conference call. The CASFO manager, Eddie Amable, opened and quietly closed the door behind him.

"Morning, thanks for coming over, Eddie."

"Morning. Have I missed anything?"

"No. We're just getting started. I'm in listen mode only for now."

Only knowing Eddie for a few months I paid careful attention to his facial expressions and body language. He was the only other manager here in this region. He'd been in Alaska about a year so he knew the ropes. Previously he was based in St. Louis as a hazmat special agent. Hazmat experience was very important in Alaska since everything, and I mean everything, gets shipped in and out of here by air. His office was located at the airport where most of the field agents were based. He was sharp and was a peer. I needed a trusted peer. Listening, occasionally jotting a note or two down, I noticed that Eddie's facial expression grew from casual to serious over the course of the telecom.

In previous meetings with him I determined that he was brilliant, scrupulously honest, diligent, fair-minded, and would set the record straight with anyone that needed setting it straight. One of the reasons I was here was because of several EEO complaints that were filed against Eddie from various agents in the office. I didn't see a manager that discriminated. I saw a manager that cared about the organization and its mission. I also saw him equally apply training, coaching, and when all else failed, discipline to ensure that the traveling public in and out of Alaska was safe. My respect for Eddie had grown by leaps and bounds in a very short time.

"That's it for now, folks. Washington out."

As the telephone lines went silent, I asked Eddie, "So what do you think?"

"Sounds like the transfer of assets and personnel is still intact but under what authority? If I heard that correctly."

Nodding, I said, "I think I heard what you did. Almost immediately after nine-eleven the Aviation and Transportation Security Act created the Transportation Security Administration as an administration of the Department of Transportation. That public law shifted the responsibility of passenger security screening from airline contract employees to federal screening. Now we're shifting again?"

"I know. This is a significant change in tactics," Eddie said. "I thought we were well into the process of meeting all of the new federal mandates. So what's the real reason behind creating a new organization within the FAA?"

"I don't know. This shift is far above our pay grades, but I have an uneasy feeling it's going to impact each and every one of us. People are going to get scared that they'll lose their jobs."

"I agree, Maggie. I agree."

Looking at my watch, "Hey, do you want to go with me to get Nelson? He's staying at the Hilton. He's going to look at our communications system and see if we can get it upgraded to at least 1995 vintage."

"No, I better get over to the CASFO. I suspect the phone lines are already burning up as the rumor mill begins."

"I'll set up a telecom for this afternoon to brief our agents on what we know so far. I'll make a few phone calls too and see if I can find anything else out. Let everyone know that I'm scheduling a telecom, let's say, for three P.M. By then I may have heard more from D.C."

"Okay."

Driving to get Nelson my mind was sorting through everything I had heard on the telecom. I was compiling all of the data, sifting through both the political posturing and what our field agents are going to react to.

Last night I told Nelson I'd come into the lobby to get him. It was way too cold to stand outside very long. I was about ten minutes early. I parked in front of the valet stand and told the attendant that I'd be right back.

Neatly dressed in dark pants, a white shirt, with a pin striped blue jacket, I quickly climbed out of my g-car, stepped up to the automatic sliding glass doors, and trotted into the lobby. I found Nelson trying to take a photo of the huge polar bear that was located just to the right of the main lobby area.

"Good morning. Impressive isn't it?"

"Sure is," Nelson said in awe.

"Look at the size of its paws. I'm glad he's not chasing us right about now."

"Me too."

"Did you have breakfast? Need coffee, anything before we head to the office?"

"No, I'm good. I got up early and came down for breakfast."

"Well, let's go then. I'm parked just outside."

Our short drive to the office was full of chit chat about when we first met in Los Angeles. He had been hired as a contract computer specialist by headquarters. He was going to be in our office for one year supporting our full time FAA employee George Wee. The government hired contract help when they could because the work was either a short term project or there wasn't enough funding to support a full time government position. The government, for the most part, at least the FAA, did not hire part-time employees. You were either full time or a contractor. Fortunately, a few years ago I had the opportunity to hire Nelson as an FAA employee. It was a wonderful opportunity for him and he was a great asset for us.

"It's great to see you, Nelson. I can't fully explain what is wrong with our communication systems except that they are slower than a tortoise and I want to confirm that they are completely secure. Our office is getting ready to take back the badging program – it's a long story – but before I accept the transfer of that data I want our system upgraded and thoroughly looked at. Pretty simple to say, but I bet not so simple to do."

"If anyone can do it, I can."

"That's one of the things I like about you. You are so positive. I know you'll solve the problem."

"Maggie, its Eddie. It's going to be an exceptionally cold night tonight and the weather forecasters are predicting a spectacular showing of the Northern Lights. Would you and Nelson be interested in seeing them?"

"Absolutely!"

"We need to leave the office around three P.M. Can you manage that today?"

"We'll make it happen. This is going to be awesome. Great idea. See you in a couple of hours, Eddie."

The three of us jumped into Eddie's SUV and headed north along Highway 1. There was still a few hours of sunlight so Nelson got the full tour of the valley north of Anchorage.

"We'll be driving towards Talkeetna, past Palmer, and north toward Denali National Park. But we won't get as far as Denali tonight. If the weather forecast is correct we're in for a good show."

"Awesome. Let's go chase some North Lights," I said gleefully.

"Buckle up. Let's go."

"I haven't been to the National Park yet. I've only seen Denali once since I've been here. You think you'd see the mountain more. I mean, Mount McKinley, which towers 20,320 feet above sea level, would be pretty hard to miss. But she's always covered in clouds."

I continued, "I remember one morning Dana came running into the office hollering for me to come with her immediately. The way she was yelling I thought someone was dying."

"Anyway, 'come on' she shouts grabbing me and dragging me to her car. Which I might add was illegally parked out in front of the building. I jumped in and she takes off like a bullet. She screeched her tires and accelerated at the same time. With the snow on the ground the car tires squealed and spun with snow spitting out before we gained traction."

Now I had Nelson and Eddie's attention.

"Well…." Eddie said.

"She drove about two blocks and stopped. She stopped in the middle of a bridge. Dana pointed out the window and said, "Look.""

At first I didn't get what she was doing or what she wanted me to see."

"See it?"

"Looking again, first at her and then out the front window I finally caught on. Denali – High One – was glistening in the morning sun. She was welcoming me to Alaska."

"Damn, girl. I didn't think I'd get here fast enough. I was driving to work from the base. When I drove across the bridge, there she was, staring at me. I knew I had to come get you, Maggie."

The driver in the car behind us honked, a short shrill honk, breaking our spell. We moved forward ever so slowly, but eventually Denali disappeared behind the tall office buildings that dotted downtown Anchorage. After we turned around to head back to the office she was already shrouded in clouds.

"That was the first and only time I've seen her since I've been here," my voice was barely a whisper and full of awe.

. . .

After driving for nearly three hours Eddie said, "Look there. On the horizon. See the lights?"

Eddie pulled off in a turn out and we all piled out of the car. It was freezing.

No, it was beyond freezing. The air was cold, crisp, our breath escaped our noses and mouths in the form of steam which immediately froze with every breath or word we spoke. But it was magnificent.

Gazing up into the night sky we could see the flowing ebbs of color as the Northern Lights danced across the pitch black night sky. The blues, green and occasionally yellow hues swirled and magically danced.

We stood outside for nearly thirty minutes watching. No words were spoken. No words could describe the beauty, the tranquility, or the magic of this event.

The bitter cold was beginning to numb our noses, fingers, and toes so Eddie reluctantly said, "Come on. Let's get back in the car. Time to warm up and head back to Anchorage."

"I'm so glad I got to see the lights," Nelson said as he rubbed his hands in an attempt to get them warmer.

I sat on my hands for a few minutes after we got back in the car.

"You know it's a magnetic storm, right?" Eddie continued, "The lights, the aurora borealis, is a storm of ionized oxygen and nitrogen atoms that play in the night skies. We were very fortunate to have clear skies tonight."

"It was magical, Eddie. I've never seen anything like it."

"Yes, it was very beautiful," Nelson said, nodding his head in agreement.

In town Eddie dropped Nelson off at his hotel first and then me.

"We're going to be wiped out later on today," I said.

"I know. Sorry about that. Didn't think the drive would take so long."

"One A.M. but well worth it. Thanks again."

"Morning, Maggie, Steven House called about ten minutes ago. He asked that you give him a call when you get in," Dana said.

"Thanks, Dana. I'll call him now."

"Thanks for calling me back so quickly," said Steven. "I spoke with Tom Thomas yesterday. He requested your assistance in western-pacific to help the region with the TSA transition. Since you were the deputy there for over five years and handled all of the personnel issues he requested that you help him and the administrative staff get prepared for the transition. As you know it's a big region, lots of field offices, and getting agents based at every Category X and 1 Airport will take some logistics to say the least. Can you spare a week a month for AWP, Maggie?"

"I'd be happy to help Tom. I'll call today and see what he needs, Steven."

"Thanks."

"Speaking of staffing, Steven. I think we should station one agent in Fairbanks. With the number of commercial, cargo, and private flights, in and out of there, we could easily support a full time employee [FTE] there. The rest of the agents can stay here in Anchorage."

"Okay, let's look into that. Send Mary an email with the justification."

"Will do."

"Okay. How's everything else going up there?"

"Things are coming together. Eddie Amable and I are working

through several of the personnel issues here. I think we're getting things under control. It's been a balancing act. Some of the agents have legitimate complaints and others don't. So we're looking at each individual's complaint on its own merit. Eddie had a solid work plan established and accountability mechanisms in place that seem logical, fair, and balanced. The regional agents and the field office agents are in sync now. I believe things are already beginning to improve."

"Good to hear. That's why you're there."

I called Tom Thomas next and reminded him that I'd see him next week.

After my conversation with Tom I began splitting my time between California and Alaska. I worked in California for two weeks and then flew up to Alaska for two weeks. The travel was exhausting, yet exhilarating. I never tired of seeing the snowcapped mountains as I flew high above Canada and into Alaska. The flight from Los Angeles to Anchorage was five and a half hours with limited food and beverage service. I was flying the route so often, the flight crew began to recognize me and greet me by name.

The two regions were distinctly different - different cultures, work environments, and personnel issues. I loved California and I now loved Alaska. I felt like Jekyll and Hyde most of the time because the issues that needed addressing for the Western-Pacific Region were completely different than those in the Alaska Region.

In Western-Pacific we established post of duty (PODs) at airports that we never had a full time presence in before. The protocol we established was to ask the agents that were already assigned to the airport if they wanted to be permanently based there. The FAA did not authorize any permanent change of station (PCS) funds, which made it more difficult for people to move, but eventually, for the most part, we got the airports staffed.

Linda and Garnetta worked tirelessly finding office space. The requests were on some unknown person's desk in D.C., but at least the requests were written and forwarded for final coordination and approval.

The Western-Pacific region had been authorized 87 field positions; 63 special agents, and 24 temporary aviation security inspectors, for distribution within California, Hawaii, Arizona, and Nevada. Cecil Forkes coordinated the moves of the staff.

Tom and I didn't have any guidance for the Singapore Office, which was also part of the Western-Pacific region, so we kept the international inspection schedules status quo and waited.

The end goal that Tom and I wanted to achieve was to have every employee in Western-Pacific stationed where they wanted to work by the time the TSA transition began. Some duty stations, for example, had more employees than needed, so we asked some agents to switch between disciplines, from internal inspections to airline and airport inspections, to justify the positions we had at those locations.

Alaska was a totally different story. The Alaska Region (AAL) only needed a staffed position in Fairbanks. Steven had already authorized that post of duty (POD), and one of the agents' stations at the ANC CASFO had already submitted paperwork for a voluntary transfer. From a personnel standpoint Alaska was simple. The twenty-one agents were all doing regulatory air carrier, airport, and hazmat work. If we needed an internal investigator I would call George Peters in Northwest Mountain and request assistance. George would have an agent fly up from the Seattle office to assist.

Summer was coming. The days were getting longer and longer. I was very proud of myself that I had survived my first winter in Alaska.

. . .

That summer I decided to take my mom to Alaska.

"Ready, Mom?"

"Oh goodie, goodie," my mom said.

After landing we collected our bags from baggage claim and

walked to my car that was parked in short term parking lot. After spending two weeks in Los Angeles I'd flown up to San Francisco. My mom lived in Novato which is less than an hour north of San Francisco. She met me at the airport and we flew together up to Alaska.

As we boarded our flight on Friday afternoon I could sense her emotions.

"I'm so excited. I get to see Alaska," she cooed.

"The flight from San Francisco to Anchorage is about four and a half hours. I got you a window seat."

Taking my hand, she reached over and kissed me on the cheek.

"We're going to have a great time, Mom."

The following Tuesday I sent an email to my brother, sister and a few of Mom's friends telling them all about the Alaska adventures we were having—such as our trip on the 26 Glacier Cruise in Prince William Sound. I had acclimated so well to the climate that I wore shorts. I thought Mom was going to faint when she saw me. I wrote about the train ride we took from Anchorage to Whittier and back. Riding the Anchorage Trolley all over town – being total tourists – loving every minute of it. We went to Lake Hood which is the largest float plane airport in the world. We went to the Earthquake Museum, which was not worth the money they charged but still interesting. And finally we drove up to Flat Top Mountain where you have a great view of Anchorage, the Knik Arm and Turn Again Arm of the Cook Inlet. I wrote about going in search of moose – and so far – we hadn't seen one.

And true to my word we were having a great time.

A week later Mom and I reversed our path and flew from Anchorage back to San Francisco. I had to part ways with her at the San Francisco Airport because I was continuing on to Oklahoma City on another flight in about an hour. I made sure she got on the Marin Airport Express which would drop her a few blocks from her home.

Steve, her neighbor, would be waiting at the bus stop to pick her up and drive her home.

"Thanks for everything, honey. It was a wonderful trip. I love you."

"I love you too, Mom. Say hi to Steve for me. I had a great time too."

After saying our goodbyes, I walked over to the Southwest Airlines gate.

On the Oklahoma City bound flight, immediately after take-off, I leaned my seat back, attempting to take a nap. The plans on taking Mom all the way home had changed after receiving an urgent telephone message from headquarters late yesterday afternoon. Headquarters was directing me to come to an emergency mandatory division managers' meeting at the Mike Monroney Aeronautical Center FAA training facility in Oklahoma City. I scrambled to find a flight out of San Francisco, middle seat, but at least I had an airline ticket.

Sleep was not going to happen. My mind swirled, my stomach churned, and my head ached as my nerves got the better of me during the four hour flight with a connection through Dallas-Fort Worth International Airport.

President George W. Bush had just announced the creation of a new Department of Homeland Security. This would be, in his words, the most significant transformation of the U.S. government in over a half-century.

The following morning, the -700s or division managers for the nine FAA security regions gathered in one of the training classrooms.

"Good morning. Thanks for flying in so quickly so we could all meet for this emergency meeting," Steven House said. "Bob Blank is going to manage the bulk of this meeting today. Bob has been working closely with Lynn Oyster at the DOT and he's going to brief us on the president's announcement that was made Tuesday. Bob."

"Morning. As you know President Bush announced the creation of the Department of Homeland Security. This is the most significant transformation of the U.S. government in over a half-century. The re-aligning of government agencies is going to be enormous."

He continued, "After careful study of the current structure, coupled with the experience gained since September eleventh and new information we have learned about our enemies while fighting a war, the president concluded that our nation needs a more unified homeland security structure."

"And what that means to us, ladies and gentlemen, is that the recently created Transportation Security Administration will eventually become part of the Department of Homeland Security."

The room exploded with comments and questions ripe with concern and confusion.

Stepping to the front of the room, Steven said, "Hold on, everyone. Please one question at a time."

"I know it makes sense. We're in a war against terrorism. Fusing together the intelligence agencies – CIA, NSA, FBI, INS, DEA, DOE, Customs, DOT – will improve the capability to identify and assess both current and future threats to the homeland," Bob said.

"What about us? What about our employees? How are we going to fit into the new organization," Bill Grover, Great Lakes division manager, demanded to know. "We're beginning to hear rumors that some Congressional leaders are being advised that FAA Security is to blame for nine-eleven and that we're becoming persona non grata."

"Everyone will have a job. That's a promise," Steven said. "Where and in what capacity, well, I don't have an answer yet, folks."

CHAPTER 19

Start of Alcoholism

"You want what?" I demanded in more than a pissed off voice.

"Please tell us your qualifications to be a Federal security director," the interviewer from the Transportation Security Administration (TSA) said to me in a dull voice.

It was prom night at Mira Costa High School. My daughter was going with a bunch of girlfriends. The limo was waiting outside as she finished getting ready. I had a seven-month-old squirmy granddaughter in my arms. I was Grandma – not a fed tonight - so I was in no mood to chat. I was looking forward to having a night away from the office, along with having some play time with my granddaughter.

Momentarily losing my temper I barked, "You want me to explain my qualifications again? This will be the third time."

"Yes."

"I've been a special agent, a first line supervisor, a manager, a deputy division manager, and a division manager with the FAA. I've been the incident command manager at multiple aviation incidents, assisted with aircraft investigations, coordinated inter-agency policy decisions, written regulations, policy, and procedures over a twenty year span. I think I'm pretty damn qualified to manage a team at one or two airports because I currently manage teams at sixteen airports spanning across four states. And, BTW, I'm currently also the division manager for FAA security for the state of Alaska. Anything else you need?"

After a brief hesitation the dull voice replied, "No, I think I've collected the information I need. We'll be in touch. Goodbye."

"Goodbye."

I hit the end button on the phone. All I wanted to do was hurl the phone across the room and scream. *So much for not having to look for a job! Every employee will transition from their same job into TSA jobs. The transition will be seamless. What a bunch of crap!*

With Miss Amber on my hip I walked over and hung up the phone, silently cursing.

The following morning the telephone rang again.

Oh great. The dull voice was back. I wonder what the hell he wants now. I sipped the coffee I had just poured.

"We're offering you a position as the Federal Security Director [FSD] at the Burbank Bob Hope Airport and Long Beach."

"That's it? No other choices," I asked.

"No. That's our offer."

"Then it looks like I'm going to Burbank."

Amazing! With all my qualifications TSA told me I have a job. Wow! And it's only thirty miles away from home.

. . .

Charlotte Biggs, one of two FAA liaisons assigned to work with TSA to assist with the management transition of FAA Security Director telephoned a few days later and asked if I would consider a possible airport switch between Burbank and Palm Springs.

"This is a huge request. I'm definitely stressing about this conversation. Burbank is a stretch, actually it's a terrible drive, but manageable. But Palm Springs, which would mean I'd need to move. Palm Springs is almost a hundred miles from my house. I'm sorry, Charlotte. I just can't."

I'm a rat. My boss, Tom's, fate is sealed. I can adjust to a thirty mile commute but not a move at this point in my life. I headed to the refrigerator to pour a glass of chardonnay. *Rat, rat, rat, I'm sorry, Tom.*

. . .

You'd think that a thirty mile commute could be done in a relatively short amount of time. Normal freeway speeds are sixty-five miles per hour. The math calculation would equate to that drive taking a half hour give or take a few minutes. But no, not in Los Angeles. The gridlock between my home in Redondo Beach and Burbank takes an hour on a good day and closer to two hours most days.

"Good morning. I'm Maggie Stewart, Federal Security Director for TSA."

"Nice to meet you. Welcome to Burbank Airport," John Daily, the airport manager, said as we firmly shook hands. "We are looking forward to working with you."

"Thanks. I'm happy to be here."

"We don't have any office space available for you or your agents yet. You can set up in the conference room for now, Miss Stewart."

"Please. Call me Maggie. Any space is fine. I really appreciate your generosity on such short notice, John."

Hoping to add a little humor, I continued," I was wondering if I was going to have to work out of my car too. I understand John Sparks, our aviation security inspector, [ASI] has been."

Smiling, John said, "I've heard that too. But now that you're here and on staff, I assume, we thought you'd need more than a Volkswagen. Come with me and I'll show you your office space. I'll have my assistant help you with your airport identification and access card too."

"Thanks."

A few minutes later we were standing in one of the airport's executive conference rooms. The west and south facing walls were windows from floor to ceiling that looked directly out onto the airfield. I felt like I was on the airfield we were so close. The view was spectacular.

"My goodness. This is a beautiful conference room."

"Well, make yourself at home. We'll probably be able to find you some office space in a few months."

"Thanks, John."

Walking in my front door at 10:00 P.M., I was exhausted but wired and wide awake. Kicking off my shoes, grabbing the mail off the glass table by the front door, I headed to the kitchen. I was starving and in need of a glass of wine.

"Hi, Mom. You're home late."

"Long day, Monica. But I suspect this will be my new work schedule. Seven days a week with fourteen hour days."

"Yikes."

"Tell me about it." I put a plate of spaghetti in the microwave, poured a glass of wine, and asked, "So how'd your day go? Culinary Arts school interesting?"

"It's really fun. I'm not real keen on cutting meat. Seafood preparation isn't much fun either. But pastries I like. I think I'm going to specialize in becoming a pastry chef."

"You can do that?"

"Yep, need to complete all of the training, all food courses, sanitation, safety, and first aid. After that you can declare a specialty and find an internship for it."

"That's great. How's Amber?"

"She's good. Finally asleep."

"Want some?" I said, pointing at the plate of steaming spaghetti.

"No thanks. I'm going back up to bed. Just wanted to see how your day went."

"Long, but good."

I sat down at the kitchen counter, opened my mail and gobbled the food. It was delicious!

"Night, Mom."

. . .

"Good morning, Cecil."

"Good morning, Maggie. You're early again, aren't you? Do you ever go home?"

"Yes," I said with a laugh, "occasionally I do."

"Okay, good. Let me get settled and I'll bring you up to speed on our hiring when you've got a few minutes."

"Sure thing. I'm here most of the morning."

. . .

"The checkpoint configuration is going to be a real challenge. We don't have enough room. The engineers are telling me that we need to widen the ticket lobby from twenty-three feet to forty-three feet. And we certainly don't have any room for offices," John said.

The new TSA Model for screening equipment isn't going to fit in the United Airlines terminal here. Terminal B is really small, Maggie."

"Well, let's sit down with the contractors later this week and see what we can do. It's all got to come together eventually. Both the new checkpoint requirements and the new checked baggage requirements require a lot more space. Burbank doesn't have a lot of terminal space to begin with, so let's see if we can map out a logical plan."

"I'll schedule a meeting," said John. "I need to follow up if we're going to get any FAA entitlement funding for these projects too. I hope we can get some Airport Improvement Plan [AIP] funding. We didn't budget for this type of expansion so I hope the feds can give us a significant amount of funding."

"I hope so too," I added. "The TSA screener hiring and training is on schedule. I'm heading down to the Marriott Hotel in Long Beach later to swear in another class of the screeners that will be used here and down at Long Beach Airport. The training for the Envision integration is going well too, John. Although I have to admit I'm not as dialed into that x-ray equipment training as I am with screening. I'll have Sparks call you. He's been working with Envision more than I have."

"Okay. He's a good guy. Two years ago, he used to work for United Airlines here. I'm glad the feds were able to hire him after he got laid off after nine-eleven. He has got tons of aviation experience."

We walked towards the security checkpoint, noting that the line to pass through security was exceptionally long this morning. The expressions on every person's face--standing with their briefcases, back backs, purses, roll bags, or newspapers--was a mix of frustration and anger.

"This is not good, Maggie. I can already see that flights are going to be delayed."

"Let me go see what's going on."

Approaching the security checkpoint I saw Sparks walking up to the checkpoint from the secured side of the terminal. He was heading directly toward the checkpoint security manager. *He had it under control.* I turned around and walked to my office.

. . .

The Marriott Hotel was adjacent the Long Beach Airport. The largest ballroom in the hotel had been contracted by TSA to use as an interview, hiring, training, and graduation facility for the newly hired and appointed federal security checkpoint screeners. When a class graduated they were sworn in by the Federal Security Director of the airport they were assigned too. Every week new screeners graduated, FSDs swore them in, and they reported for duty. At each airport a TSA manager assigned to manage the checkpoint operations handled everything from assisting in the configuration of each checkpoint, the staffing, and on-the-job training for each screener.

"Let me introduce you to the graduates," Carman the director for screener training said as he led me to the podium.

As we walked to the front of the room, heads turned and looked at both Carman and me.

Carman Luis had been hired by TSA to oversee the training facility for the Burbank and Long Beach Airports. He was short, stocky, but appeared fit. His voice carried a pleasant yet commanding tone, rich with an Italian accent. He didn't walk to the podium, he stream rolled to it. His introduction was brief and to the point.

After the applause subsided I said, "Good afternoon, ladies and gentlemen. I cannot thank you enough for wanting to serve your country in this capacity. Being a TSA security screener means that you are the first line of defense in making sure the traveling public is safe. Always remember the importance of your jobs with every bag you search. Only you can prevent a hijacking from occurring or a bomb from getting onboard an airplane."

Once the room quieted for the second time, "Now please stand to be sworn in as federal screening personnel."

. . .

After the swearing in ceremony I drove to the Long Beach Airport to see how things were progressing there. Driving up to the tiny airport brought a smile to my face. When I was young, my sister, brother, and I would fly from Long Beach to San Francisco a few times a year to visit our mom. My mom moved there after our parents divorced. I didn't understand any of the friction between my parents back then. I just knew that I loved getting on airplanes, sitting by the window, and gazing down toward the ground as the clouds swirled and floated past me. I felt free. I knew the moment that I stepped onto an airplane that somehow, someway, someday I was going to be involved in aviation.

Walking into the main terminal I felt my heart warm and I smiled. Most of the dark blue industrial carpet had been removed because of the security checkpoint construction. Underneath the dull, dingy, ugly carpet lay the most beautiful mosaic patterns of tile. As I stepped onto a sun design I wondered why anyone would cover up this incredible artistry.

I loved this tiny, relatively unchanged, antique airport. Five airlines flew to and from here. When I saw the exquisite tile from past days I was even more in love with its quaint beauty.

The checkpoint expansion was coming along but unfortunately the limited size of the airport property had curtailed the ability to put what we wanted into the cargo screening areas. Our solution was to erect huge tent structures. They were placed on the backside of the passenger terminal facing the airline ramp. The airport terminal was a historic landmark and could not be altered in any way. You couldn't see this airport modification from the front of the terminal but after you cleared screening it was very unsightly.

It wasn't beautiful by any means but it met our federal mandate. *It will be okay for now, Maggie. We'll figure out more permanent solutions later. Let's just meet the target installation and implementation dates.*

I walked in the front door, kicked off my shoes, and headed for the refrigerator. I was hungry, thirsty, and tired. But I was thrilled to see everything coming together. From airport managers to ramp agents the cooperation, the teamwork, the can-do spirit was visible every day. No one, not one single person in the aviation community, ever wanted to see another day like 9.11.

· · ·

"I have to say this is the most stressful job I've ever had," I said to Agent Stanton. "But one of the most rewarding too."

"I know. TSA is FAA Security on steroids. The 'managers'– us - we're under tremendous pressure to stand this organization up."

"And we're doing it! I just need more hours in the day, as if fourteen-hour work days aren't enough."

"I hear you. I'm lucky I'm still at LAX, but that won't last forever. Don't get me wrong, Dave Strong is a terrific Federal Security Director. And being the AFSD for inspections is right up my alley here at LAX, but I've got my sights on other jobs in TSA. I want my own airport again someday, Maggie."

"Yep, I can't understand the decision to put you at a lower level at LAX except for the idea that politics is sometimes more powerful than logic. I know all of the Category X Airports were on the political chopping block. The former FAA federal security directors never had a chance. No one knows LAX Airport like you do."

"Damn straight."

"Any press issues at LAX?"

"Sure are. The press is curious. Unfortunately they are looking for negative news stories. I can keep them away from the checkpoint until they buy a ticket to fly. Then there isn't a damn thing I can do except prevent them from taking pictures."

"Agreed. We had one journalist arrested last week because she wouldn't stop taking pictures at the checkpoint. LAX PD officers were irate."

"And the law enforcement issues are mounting. The cops don't like the National Guard presence. But we both know the airports don't have enough law enforcement to monitor the checkpoints, ticket counters, boarding gates, cargo security, and still have roving patrols."

"I think the National Guard is here for the long haul, Maggie."

"Me too. And D.C. management is on our backs directing us that we absolutely make sure our agents don't supervise at the checkpoints, but our ASIs can."

"Fine line between supervising and monitoring," Agent Stanton said with a wink. "But remember our ASIs came from an aviation background. Most of our agents came from a law enforcement background, which is HQ's rationale."

"It's logical, but difficult to accomplish sometimes. If it's this crazy at Burbank with only three checkpoints I can't imagine what it's like there at LAX."

"Don't ask."

"Don't worry I won't. I've got to go. Telecom with D.C. in about fifteen minutes."

Sitting at my desk, the phone mute button turned on, I quickly checked my emails while waiting for the telecom to begin.

"Good afternoon, everyone. Steven here. We've got a lot of ground to cover today, folks. On the administrative side we're still working on finalizing position descriptions, pay bands, and office policies to ensure that we have consistency across the country. I understand the need for office space where FSDs are located. So far we have 2,460 leases to review and two people here in D.C. doing that! That means – patience – new office space isn't going to happen overnight."

"AUO, administratively uncontrolled overtime, regional staffing, and what we're going to do with the dangerous goods program is still under discussion at the department level. Like I said, everything is a work in progress.

"However, the good news is that the screening checkpoint hiring and checkpoint equipment modifications are on track. Every airport in the country now has federal screeners working at them. It's been a huge undertaking but each and every one of you have made that happen."

You could hear clapping in the background as Steven paused before continuing.

"Now, we won't be seeing any early buy-outs for retirement. I know that rumor has been floating around but TSA says they need our corporate memory so they are not authorizing any early retirements. So get used to the pace, ladies and gentlemen. Stay well, rest when you can, but keep going. You're all doing a fantastic job."

"Fantastic job," *now that was good to hear,* I whispered to myself as I accelerated to join the flow of traffic on the I-5 freeway. "We're doing a fantastic job, and we have fantastic jobs," I suddenly shouted out loud. It's incredible and an honor to be directly involved in the transformation of aviation security. I couldn't have a more important or powerful job.

Thanking God for a safe ride home, I turned into my driveway at 8:33 P.M. I was tired, hungry, and thirsty. *A glass of chardonnay was in my immediate future.*

Be careful, Maggie. Long days, long hours, lots of stress, and not much sleep may turn the Transportation Security Administration [TSA] into The Start of Alcoholism [TSA] for me. A TSA I don't need.

CHAPTER 20

Picture on the Piano

"Good golly, Maggie. Another marvelous drive up the one-ten free-way. I can't wait," I sang, totally off key, at the top of my lungs, as KNX 1070 radio barked out to me that I was totally screwed. It was 5:15 A.M., a big-rig jack-knifed and crashed at 2:00 A.M, closing all lanes. Three hours later the car pool lane was open but the rest of the freeway was a mess. I was not thrilled. My car was barely moving along thirty-three miles of clogged, smoggy pre-dawn traf-fic congestion, and I was stuck with nowhere to go.

"And guess what, Maggie," I sang even louder, "it's the only frigging route to Burbank Airport, at least, the only route I know. Shit."

Two hours later, when I arrived late for work, the office was buzzing with activity.

"Good morning," Cecil said when I walked in the door.

"You think? The commute was a pain today. You? Did you get here on time?"

With a sly grin, Cecil said, "Well, maybe…"

"Nice to see you too," I said as I marched to my office.

Browsing at my inbox I saw the paperwork for John Sparks, to be converted from a temporary employee to permanent employment with TSA. Cecil reminded me last week that several of the aviation security inspectors were off probation and it was time for me to decide if they should be converted to permanent employees.

John was a jolly, full-sized guy, with graying hair at his temples, blue eyes. He wore glasses most of the time. He was with United Airlines for over twenty years before being laid off shortly after 9.11. It was a terrible blow to him and his family both financially and emotionally. When a person is with a company for many years there is usually some loyalty by the company in return for your years of service. Unfortunately, United Airlines had a different sense of appreciation for John and hundreds of other employees.

He wasn't always calm. Sometimes he barked orders, momentarily losing his temper, which always prompted me to invite him for a coffee. Sipping our coffee we would chat about teamwork and the importance of remaining calm at work.

"I understand the concept, Maggie," he once said to me. "It's just hard executing the technique."

Faults and all, I also recognized and appreciated his aviation experience. John had credibility with the station managers here. He was a known commodity to them which, in part, made the transition from private to federal screening for the airlines at Burbank relatively easy.

For me the current stressor was finding office space. The airport expansion needs - checkpoints, checked baggage, and cargo screening, all federally required, had pushed our office off airport property because there was not enough room onsite. It was ironic that we, the federal agency responsible for the increased security expansion were the first to be forced to find offices off the airport property. In a way I found it humorous. *Now we'll need to get in a g-car and drive to every meeting, inspection, and ad-hoc visit at the airport.* Yet, somehow I imagine the airport and airline station managers were smiling. Smiling, because it would limit our constant oversight of them.

John Sparks found the office space we were looking at. The drive was less than ten minutes, plenty of parking for our staff, and it was easy to find. The federal purse strings were open. Leasing office space was relatively easy compared to the normal bureaucratic snail's pace. Nine-eleven sped up the process a hundred fold.

When John suggested we procure this office space, Cecil and I balked at the idea. Balked because the space was gorgeous, large, and expensive. It was more office space that I had ever procured so I was cautious.

"Cecil, can we do this? Can you get a lease on this building for us?"

"I think we can, Maggie. TSA has control of the checkbook and the backload is horrendous, but I think the money is there. Let me see what I can do."

With those thoughts in mind I quickly signed the bottom of the SF-52, sealing John's future with TSA.

. . .

Six weeks later the office was ours. TSA was moving into a movie studio!

Burbank is known for movie studios and movie stars. For me the commute was a painful waste of time, but the charm and energy of the area was infectious. It was upbeat and alive. When I was young, my mom and dad lived and worked in Hollywood. Hollywood movie studios are located in Burbank. My parents both had jobs with Hollywood connections – so it was somehow fitting, for me, anyway, that we found an empty Burbank movie studio for our TSA office.

The office was modern, spacious, open, and invigorating.

"It's perfect. Look we can even roller skate!"

"What?"

"Look, the entire outer office space has cement flooring – look it's a circle, and it goes all the way around the office. See the circle in the center? And, look, the window sections are carpeted. The cement flooring goes around in an entire circle. Think how fast we'll be able to meet with one another if we're all on roller skates!"

No sense of humor in this room, that was for sure.

At both Long Beach and Burbank the security checkpoint re-con-figurations were complete, the new federal security screeners were in place. The x-ray facilities for checked baggage and some cargo screening had been accomplished by erecting huge permanent tents on the back side of the main terminal area.

After seeing the cargo facility construction at Burbank for the first time, I said, "It resembles a circus tent."

"This was the only way we could accomplish having an additional ten thousand feet for all of the screening functions here," Jerry Snyder, from the airport building department, said with a slight tone of disgust.

"I know, Jerry. I didn't mean to offend you. You're doing a marvelous job under really difficult circumstances."

Jerry shrugged, grunted, and walked away.

Good going, Maggie. You just upset a man who's worked very, very hard.

"Hey, Jerry. Wait up," I said as I trotted after him to apologize.

. . .

Several months after starting to work out of the Burbank office, I practically leaped across my desk to grab the ringing telephone. "Transportation Security Administration, Maggie Stewart," I answered.

"Hi Maggie. Steven House here."

"Hi. How are you? Heard through the grapevine that you've been pretty sick."

"Better now. Thanks for asking. Doctors told me to slow down a notch or two. Easier said than done, but I'm trying."

"With this pace. I can't even imagine what an eight hour workday is anymore."

"Absolutely. I haven't seen one of those since nine-eleven. Most of us haven't. But I've got a proposal that might shorten your work days just a tad if you're interested."

"Sure, I'm listening."

"As you know we've been in a lengthy discussion with TSA and Homeland Security about how to allocate all of our full time employee [FTE] positions between FAA and TSA. TSA wanted to take every position we had in security and laterally transfer them across to their organization."

"Yes, I remember hearing that."

"TSA wanted all of our people, but not all of our job functions."

He paused. "But Lynn and I have been strongly opposed to that because it would completely deplete every security asset in the FAA. Our personnel security specialists, facility security folks, internal investigations, every position – leaving the FAA without any internal security infrastructure. And TSA has no idea about the complexity of the hazardous materials program."

"Okay."

"Yesterday TSA and the FAA struck a deal. That deal kept an internal security element and the hazardous materials program within the FAA."

"That's terrific, Steven. Congratulations."

"Yes, we're extremely pleased. There are some field folks that are very pleased too. With a segment of our organization remaining with the FAA we're in need of some additional leadership. I'd like to offer you the Western-Pacific division manager's job with a ten percent pay increase effective immediately."

"Really? Yes, I'd love to come back to the FAA but there's more to be done here."

"We understand that, Maggie, but we're up against a tight hiring schedule here. If we don't fill the vacancies ASAP we'll lose them. That's the agreement we made with TSA. We need you to decide now."

"Okay, I understand. I need to tell my staff first. I owe them so much. We've been practically living together for the last sixteen months. They are going to be devastated."

"I know. It can't be helped. What do you say?"

"Yes. I'd be honored to return to the FAA."

"Great. We're looking forward to putting your picture back on the piano."

Epilogue

After leaving the Transportation Security Administration and rejoining the Federal Aviation Administration, I continued working for another ten years. I retired, in January 2013, after 31 years of service.

It was an honor and a privilege to protect, defend, and serve my country.

Acknowledgements

Thank you support team:

Bernard and Sylvia Dietsch

Troy and Monica Lyons

Michael and Toni Noaker

Ron and Roberta Pelayo

Tim and Marilyn Sawyer

Andrew and Cathy Strabella

Disclosures

Each chapter was re-created from personal notes and memory. The names were intentionally changed to preserve their anonymity.

Also By Madelyn I. Sawyer

Hired to Protect: Adventures of a Federal Air Marshal

Hired to Defend: The Second Book of The Adventures of a Federal Air Marshal

Hired to Serve: The Final Book of The Adventures of a Federal Air Marshal

CPSIA information can be obtained at www.ICGtesting.com
Printed in the USA
BVOW01s2343150315

391797BV00002B/4/P

9 781478 752837